whose beginning is not,
nor end cannot be

whose beginning is not, nor end cannot be

Ulla von Brandenburg

Irish Museum of Modern Art/
Áras Nua-Ealaíne Na hÉireann

CHARTA

Tarot: Roy de Deniers (King of Coins), 2008

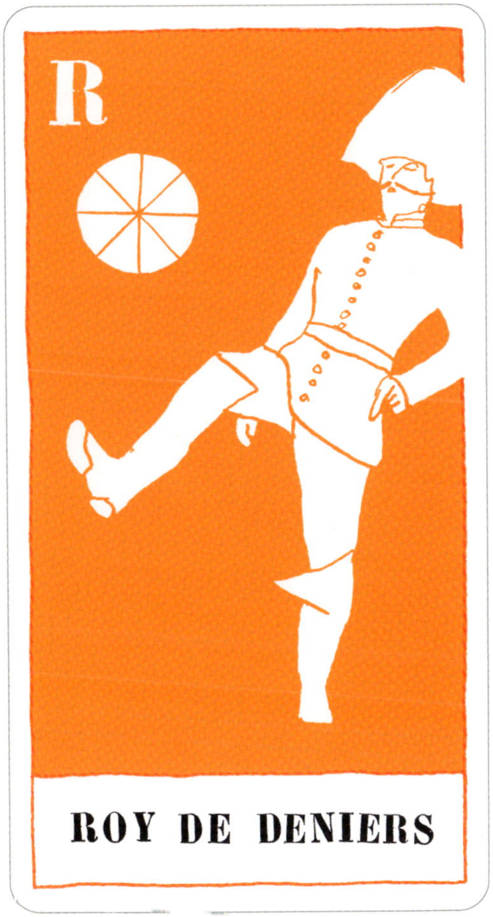

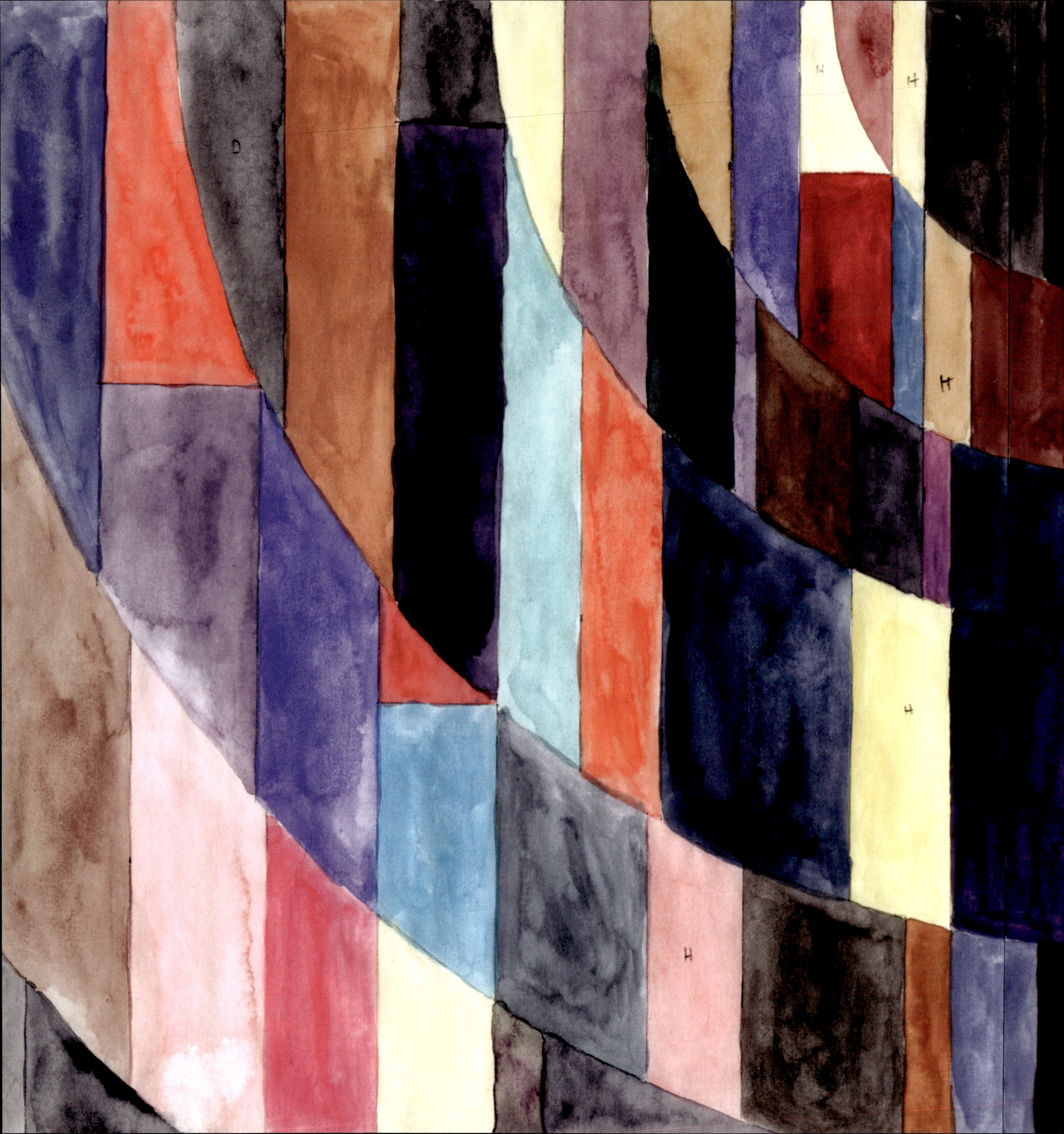

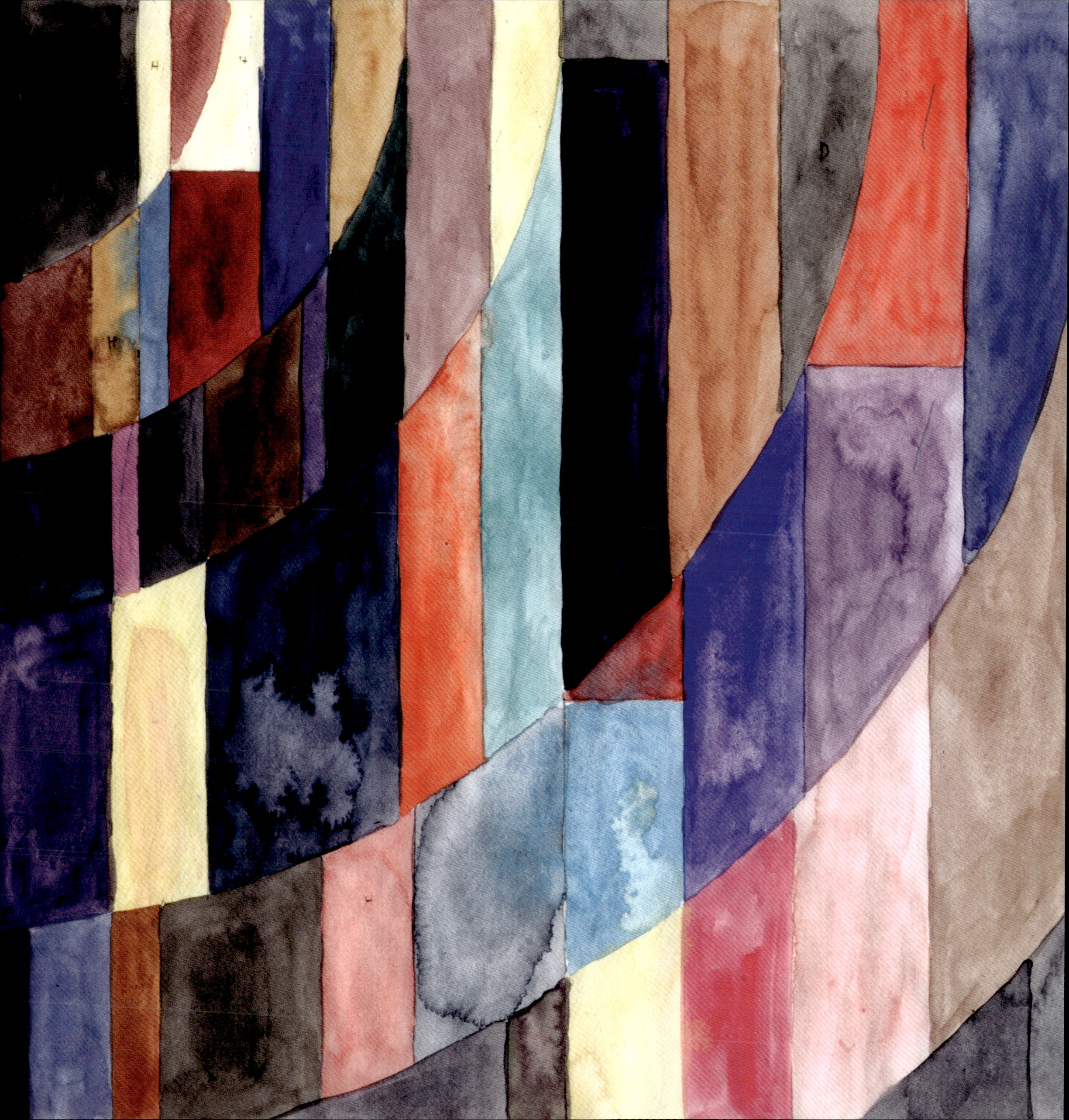

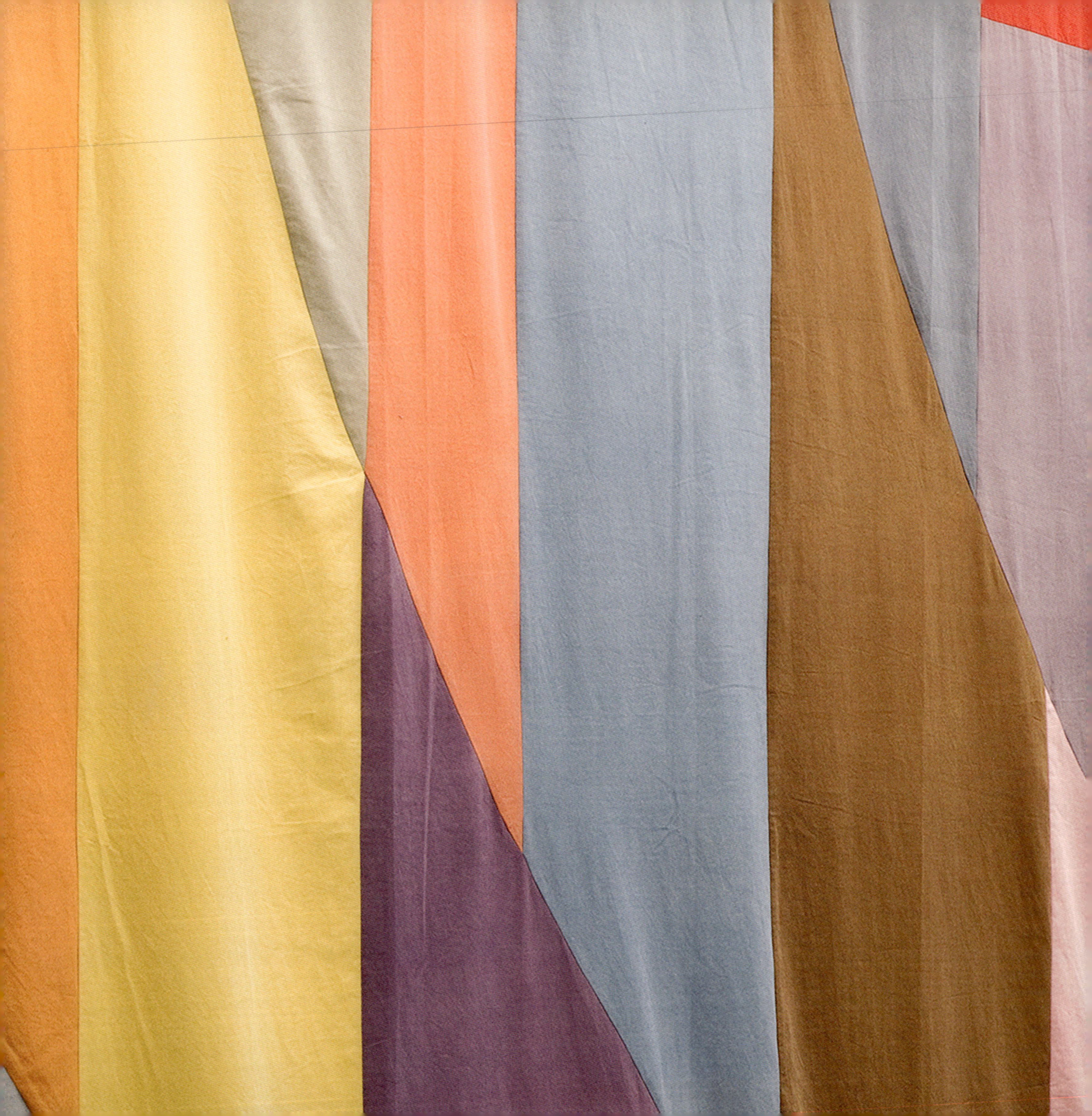

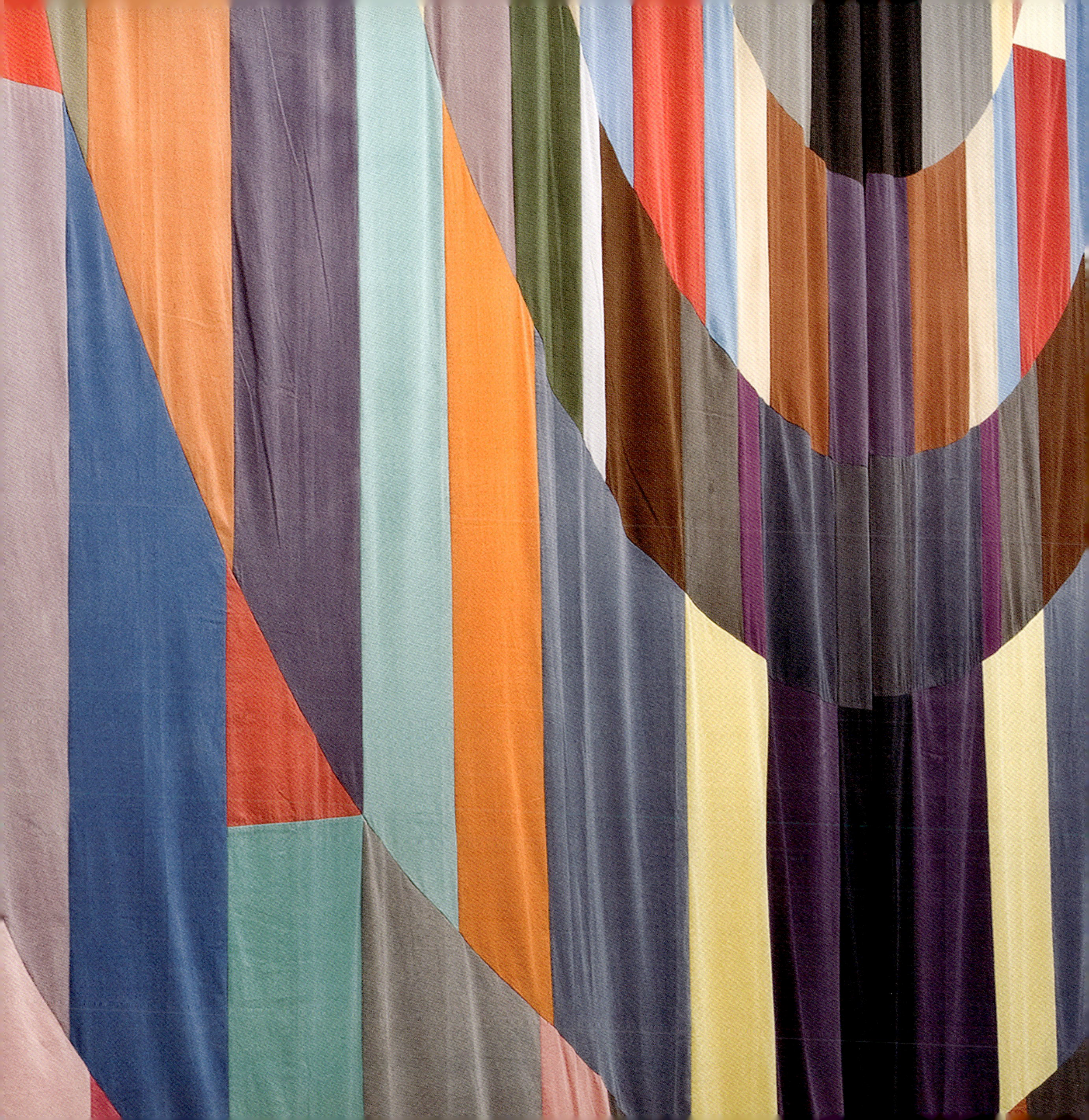

Published on the occasion of the exhibition
Ulla von Brandenburg
whose beginning is not, nor end cannot be
27 May — 12 October 2008

Exhibition curated by Rachael Thomas:
Senior Curator; Head of Exhibitions

IMMA Exhibition Team:
Enrique Juncosa: Director
Rachael Thomas: Senior Curator; Head of Exhibitions
Nicola Lees: Assistant Curator; New Galleries
Cillian Hayes: Head of Technical Staff
Gale Scanlan: Head of Operations
Georgina Jackson: Project Curator
Lucia Pietroiusti: Project Assistant

Editor: Nicola Lees; Assistant Curator; New Galleries
Associate Editor: Rachael Thomas; Senior Curator; Head of Exhibitions
Copy Editors: Charlotte Bonham-Carter, Tom Cobbe, Brian Cass and Georgina Jackson
Translator: Susan Cox
Catalogue and typeface design: A2/SW/HK, London

Charta Team:
Editorial Coordination: Gabriele Nason, Daniela Meda, Filomena Moscatelli
Copywriting and Press Office: Silvia Palombi Arte&Mostre, Milano
US Editorial Director: Francesca Sorace
Promotion and Web: Monica D'Emidio
Distribution: Antonia De Besi
Administration: Grazia De Giosa
Warehouse and Outlet: Roberto Curiale

British Library Cataloguing in Publication Data.

A catalogue record for this book is available from the British Library.

ISBN 978-88-8158-693-6

Printed in Italy
in May 2008
by Tipografia Rumor, Vicenza

Irish Museum of Modern Art/
Áras Nua-Ealaíne Na hÉireann
Royal Hospital, Military Road
Kilmainham, Dublin 8, Ireland
Tel +353 1 612 9900
Fax +353 1 612 9999
e: info@imma.ie
www.imma.ie

Edizioni Charta srl
Milano
via della Moscova, 27 - 20121
Tel +39-026598098/026598200
Fax +39-026598577
e-mail: edcharta@tin.it

Charta Books Ltd.
New York City
Tribeca Office
Tel +1-313-406-8468
e-mail: international@chartaartbooks.it

To find out more about Charta,
and to learn about our most recent
publications, visit
www.chartaartbooks.it

Contents

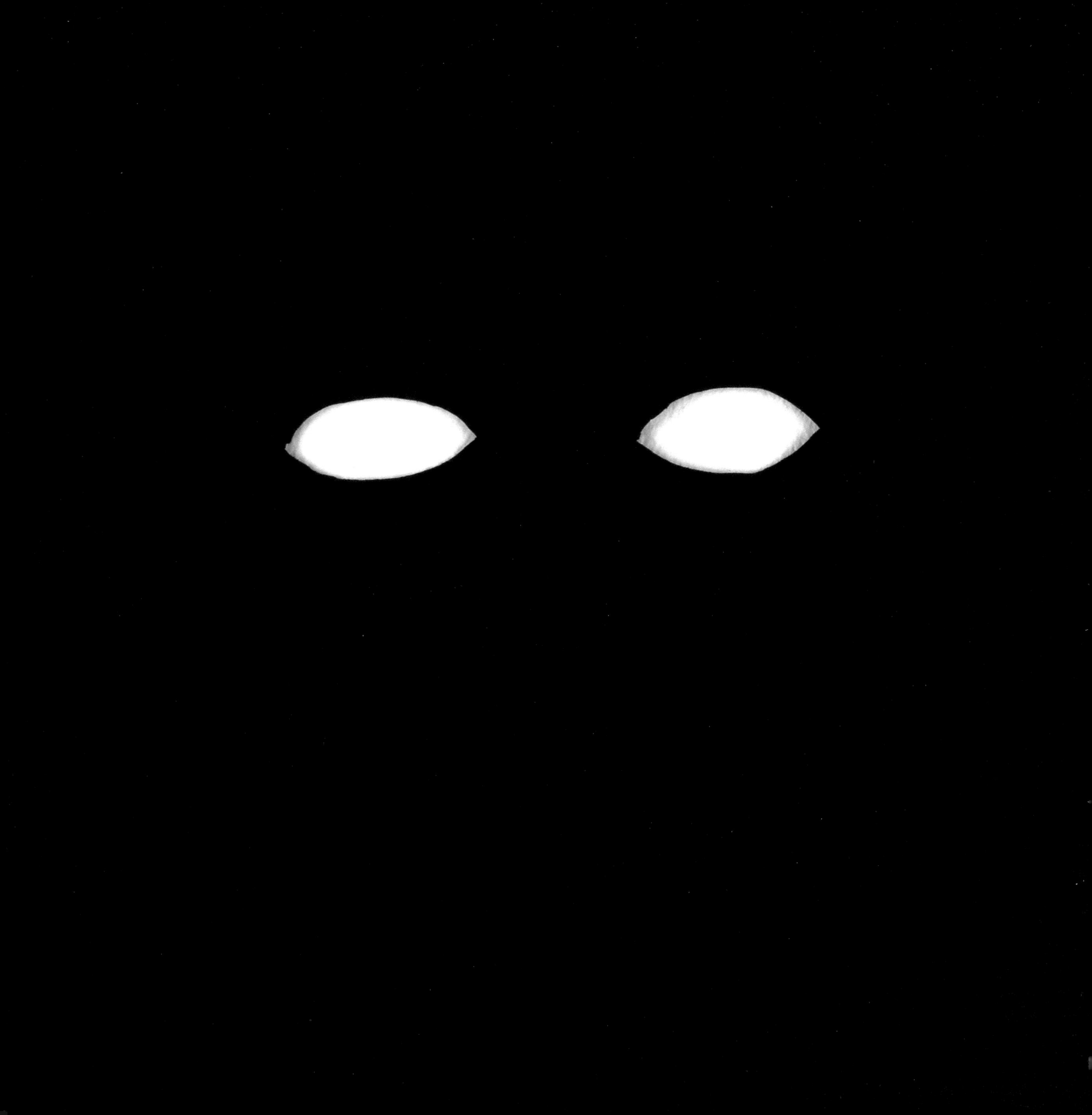

Foreword

The Irish Museum of Modern Art is proud to present the first solo exhibition in Ireland by the innovative young German artist Ulla von Brandenburg. Curated by Rachael Thomas, *whose beginning is not, nor end cannot be*, is an exhibition of recent and newly commissioned works, which surveys a wide range of media including film, drawing, installation and performance. The exhibition reflects the imaginative loops through time, elastic conceptions of history, and recurring themes that characterise Brandenburg's work, and are subtly, yet rigorously, weaved together throughout her practice.

For her exhibition at IMMA, Brandenburg draws upon certain devices from theatre to investigate the meaning of performance. Noticeably, the entire external wall of IMMA's East Ground galleries is adorned with a theatre curtain. As you pass the curtain, you are unsure what side you are supposed to be on. Are you on the side of the actors or the audience? The curtain is a visual mechanism that is borrowed from a scene in Buñuel's film *The Discreet Charm of the Bourgeoisie (Le charme discret de la bourgeoisie)* (1972). In the film, a group of people sit around a table when suddenly, a wall – or what appears to be a wall – opens up to reveal a gathering of spectators watching the scene unfold. According to Brandenburg, the people around the table '...are no longer subjects, but objects of the spectator's gaze.' In her practice, Brandenburg explores the immediacy of theatre and performance, and the ability of the live act to create meaning out of the mundane. Unlike other media, theatre exists only as it is performed, constituting a unique experience that cannot be preserved through documentation, or restaging.

The 'spaces' explored in this exhibition are the thresholds beyond, between and past, reality and artifice. Brandenburg finds inspiration in a myriad of historical elements sourced from literature, visual art, expressionist theatre, Hollywood films, chess, and magic, as well as pre-Freudian psychoanalysis. The common thread amongst these disparate influences, however, is always the suggestion of the existence of a world between the reality and the artifice. It comes as no surprise that Brandenburg studied both set design and visual arts in Karlsruhe and at the Hamburg School of Fine Arts.

Many of Brandenburg's installations present uncertainty; it is not clear if the show is over, or whether the performance has just began. This condition is reflected in the exhibition's title, *whose beginning is not, nor end cannot be*, a quote taken from an Angelic Conversation conducted by Magus John Dee (1527—1609), a noted mathematician, astronomer, astrologer, geographer, occultist, and consultant to Queen Elizabeth I. Magus Dee, who devoted much of his life to alchemy, divination, and Hermetic philosophy, was an extremely influential Elizabethan intellectual force, whose pursuit of truth sometimes led to great illusions and folly. It is commonly thought that the character Prospero in William Shakespeare's *The Tempest* and Christopher Marlowe's Dr Faustus are both based upon the Elizabethan scholar.

Brandenburg's form of alchemy begins as the visitor passes through the theatre curtain outside the East Ground galleries of IMMA. Passing over the threshold of the exhibition stage, the visitor encounters four rooms that are presented as individual chapters, which also form the structure of this book. In the first room of the exhibition, there are a number of works on paper, and a newspaper, No 4, which is based upon a Danish photo-book. Following, in the second room, is a nocturnal wall drawing, designed specifically for IMMA. The work *Karo Sieben* (Seven of Diamonds, 2007) fills the third room, while the fourth room – and the final chapter – consists of the 16mm film work, *8* (2007), which depicts recurring themes in Brandenburg's practice. The film's narrative is constructed through a single shot that gently pans and flows through a French castle inhabited by all the tableaux vivants from Brandenburg's past works, threading together numerous theatrical scenes and layering characters, such as chess players, ghosts and a sleeping man.

Throughout the exhibition, Brandenburg repeatedly returns to materials, such as regalia ribbons, gentlemens' ties and canes, which mark the late 19th Century, and the transition to so-called Modernity. She uses the period's "cultivated" appearances and image ideas as a formal filter when discussing contemporary collective experiences.

As part of this exhibition, we are delighted that Brandenburg will present a new shadow play in the IMMA chapel. In this catalogue we have reproduced Act 3 of Anton Chekov's play, 'The Cherry Orchard' (c.1904). This draws out the relationship between theatre as a constructed space and theatre as text mirroring the important concerns that are imbedded in Brandenburg's performances. 'The Cherry Orchard' investigates socio-economic conditions, and the rise of the middle class, in Russia at the turn of the 20th Century.

Born in Karlsruhe, Germany, in 1974, Ulla von Brandenburg currently lives and works in Hamburg. Recent solo exhibitions include Kunstverein, Düsseldorf; Art:Concept, Paris, 2007; Produzentengalerie Hamburg, 2007; Palais de Tokyo, Paris, 2006; and Kunsthalle Zürich, 2006. Group exhibitions in 2007 include *Performa 07*, Performa, New York; *The World as a Stage*, Tate Modern, London; *Against Time*, Bonniers Konsthall, Stockholm; 3rd Prague Biennial, and *Pale Carnage*, Arnolfini Gallery, Bristol.

The production of an exhibition is always a collaborative undertaking and I would firstly like to thank the curator of this exhibition Rachael Thomas (Senior Curator: Head of Exhibitions), Nicola Lees (Assistant Curator: New Galleries), Georgina Jackson (Project Curator) and Lucia Pietroiusti (Project Assistant), as well as our team at IMMA. I would like also to acknowledge the assistance of Rolf Stehle and Barbara Ebert from the Goethe-Institute, Dublin, who kindly sponsored this exhibition; the artist's galleries, Art:Concept, Paris, Produzentengalerie, Hamburg and Pilar Corrias Ltd, London; the designers of the catalogue Scott Williams and Henrik Kubel at A2/SW/HK, London; as well as the Irish writer Declan Long and the internationally renowned curator Beatrix Ruf, who gave Ulla von Brandenburg one of her first exhibitions at the Kunsthalle, Zurich, for their insightful texts. Finally, and most importantly, we would like to thank Ulla von Brandenburg for her vision and enthusiasm in developing this exhibition.

Enrique Juncosa
Director

Tarot: 9 de Deniers (9 of Coins), 2008

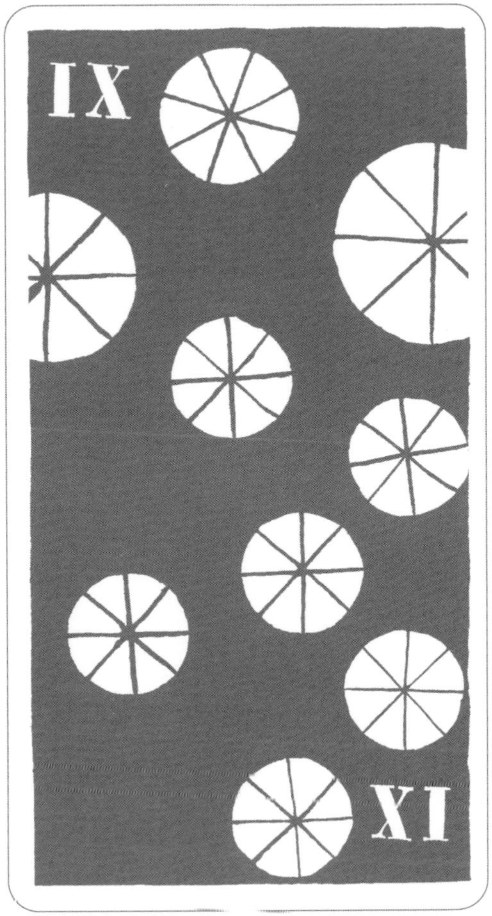

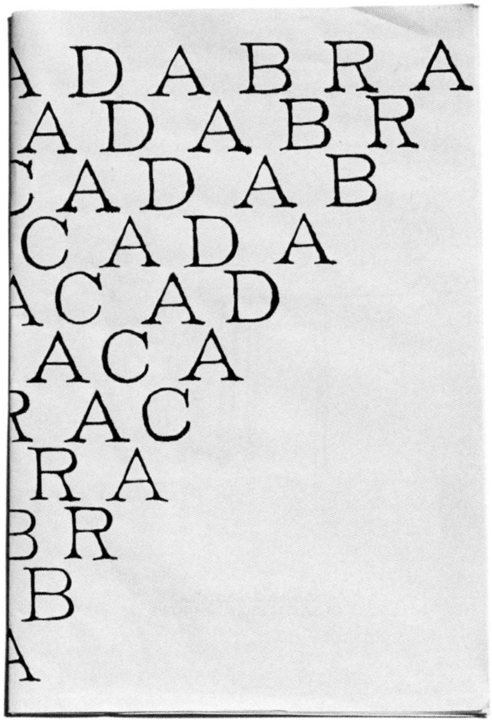

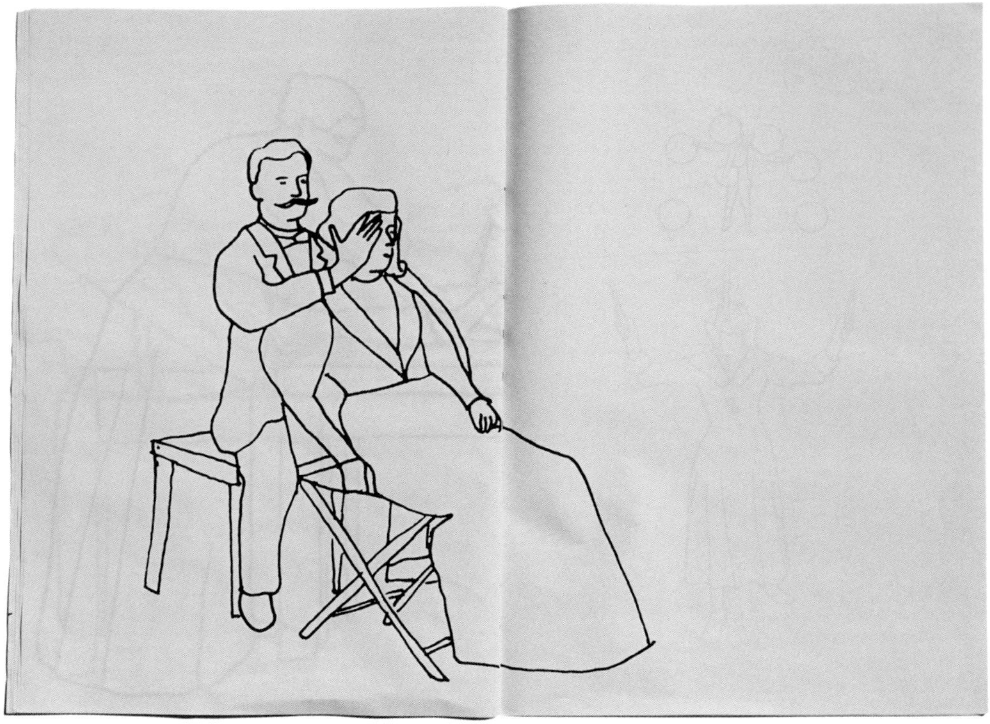

Abracadabra, 2002

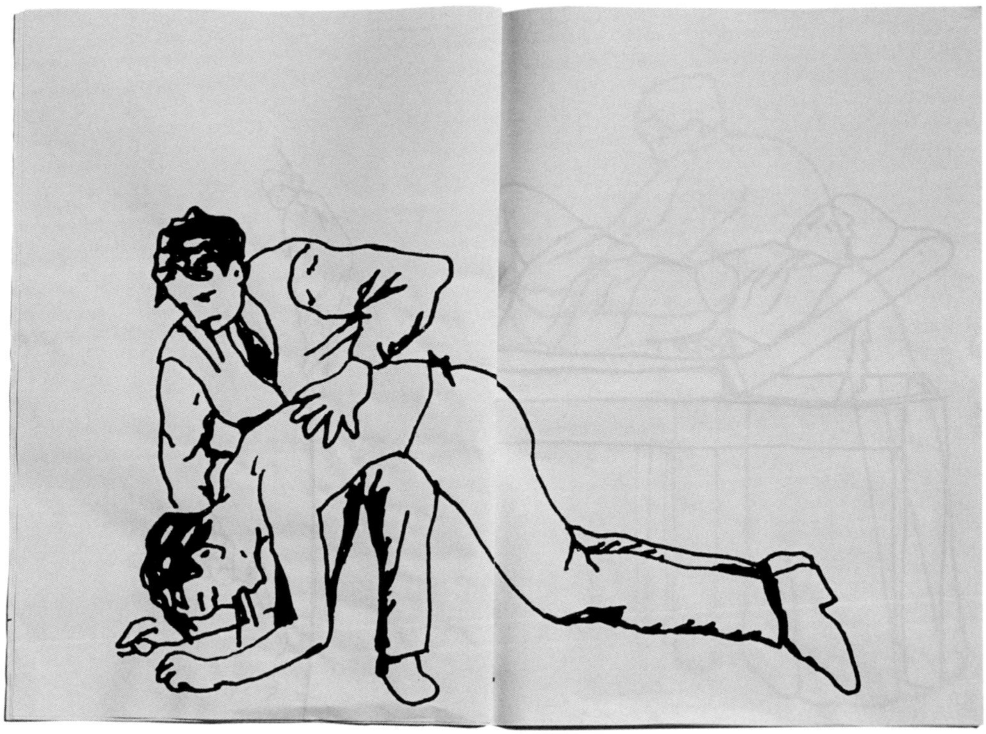

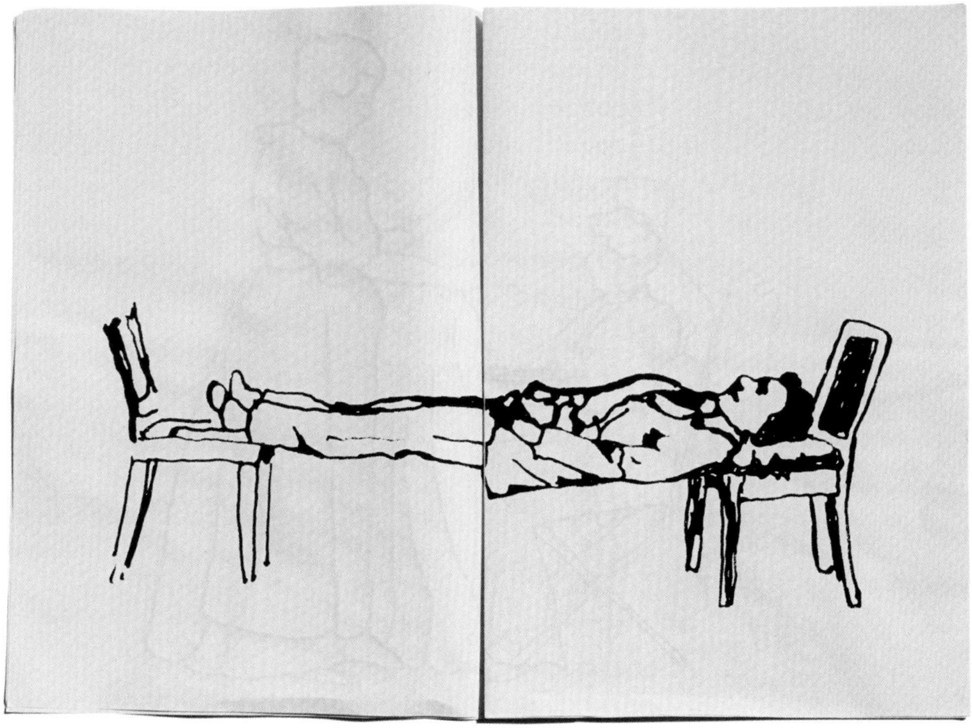

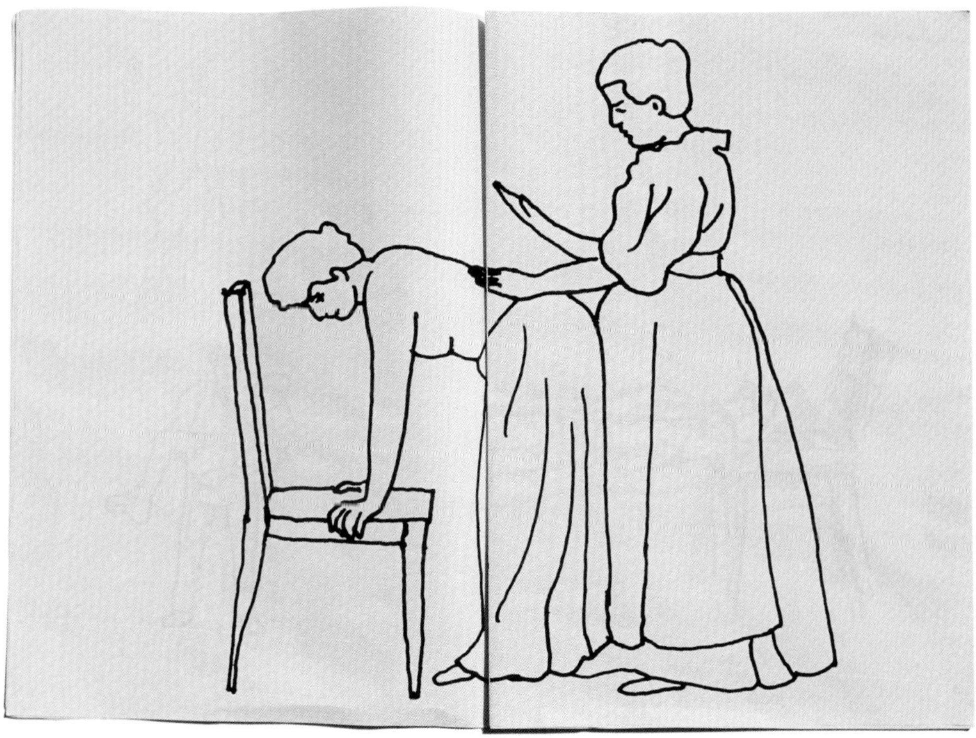

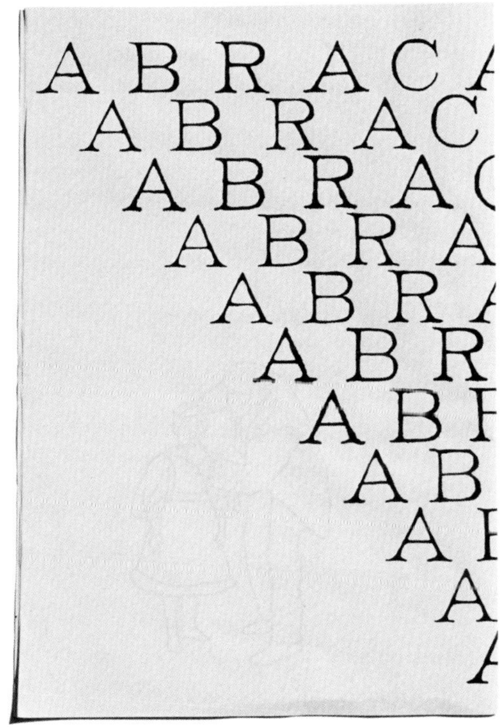

5 | Ulla von Brandenburg

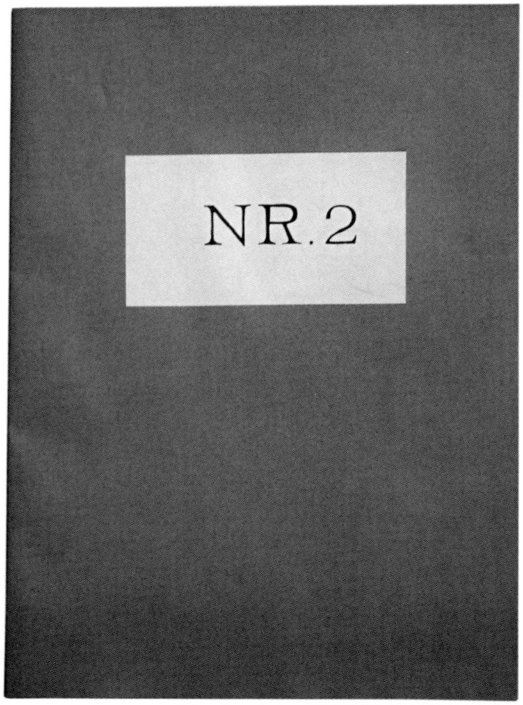

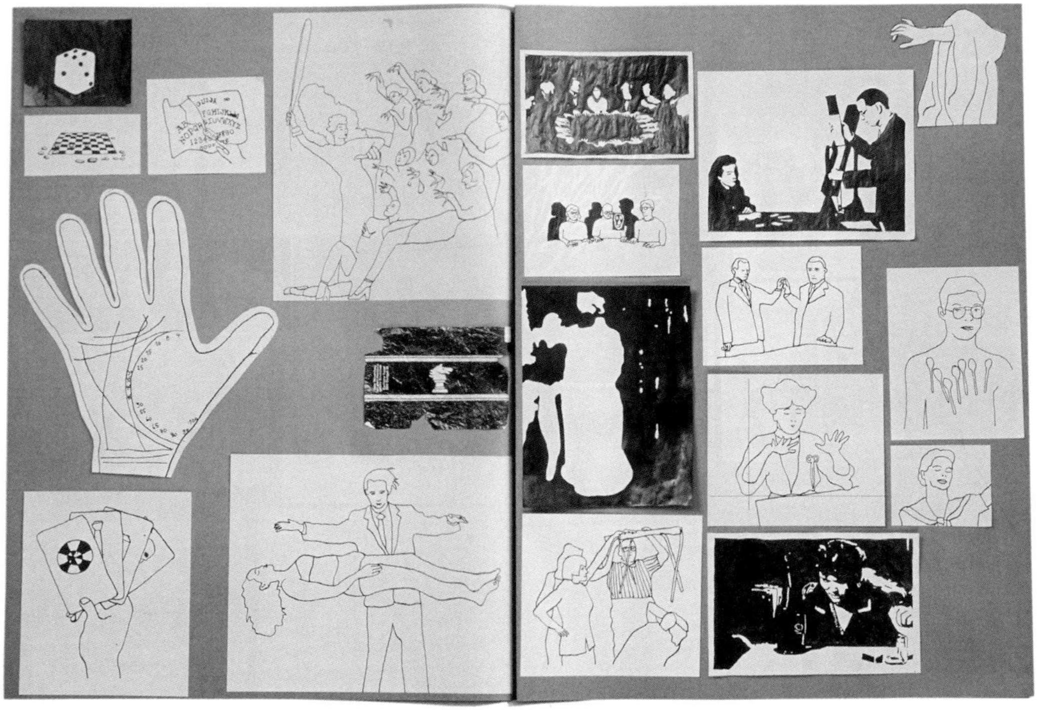

NR.2, 2004

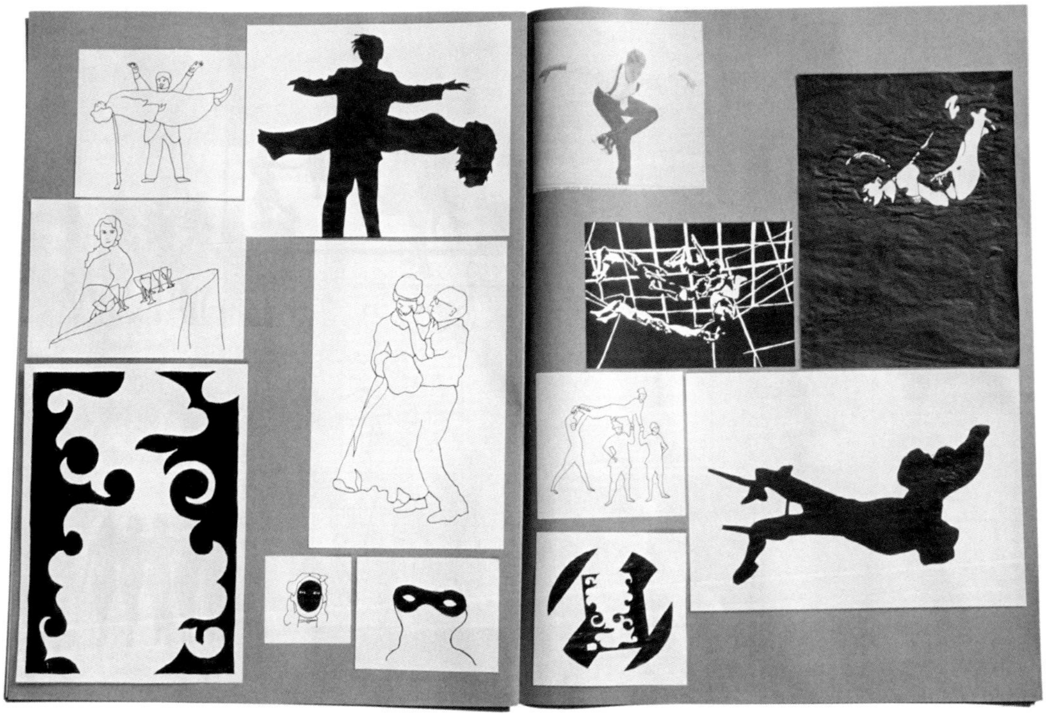

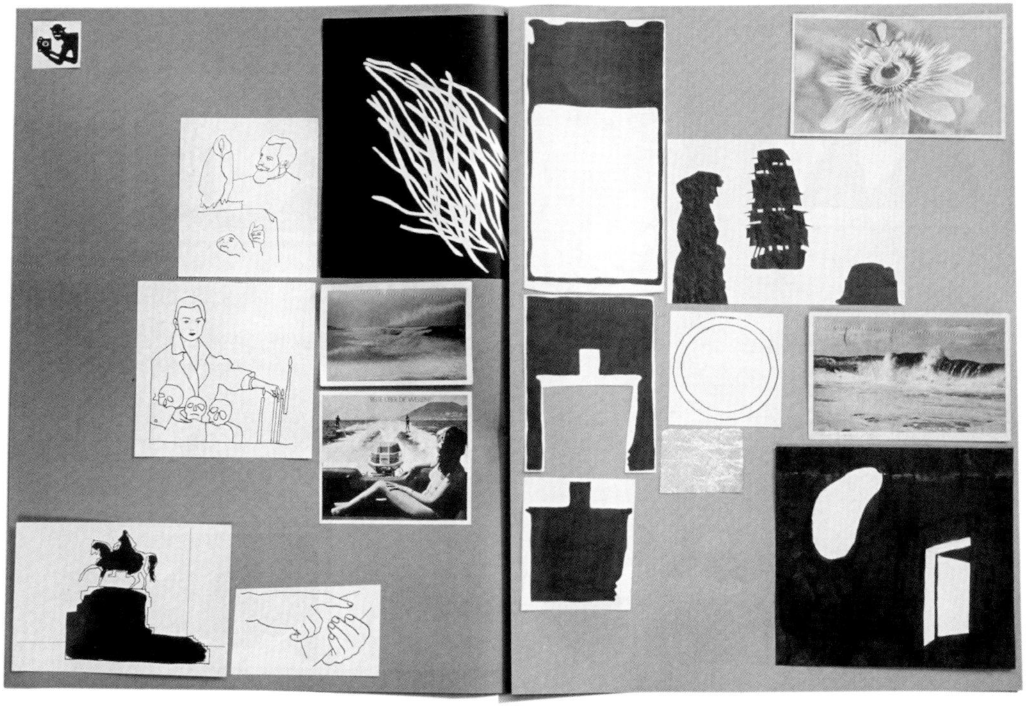

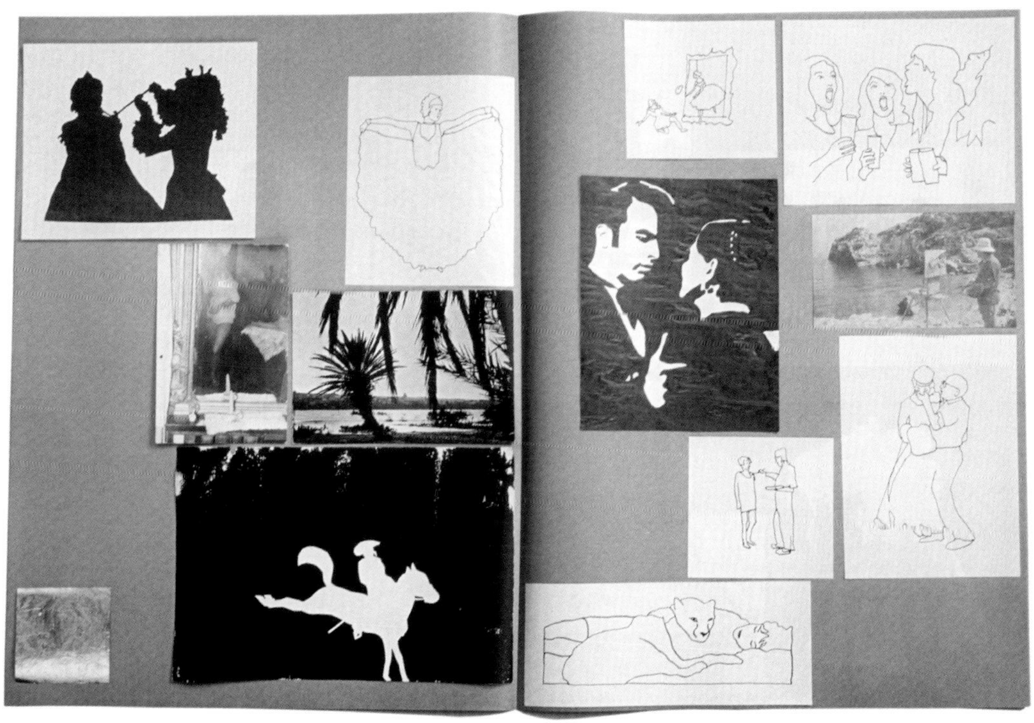

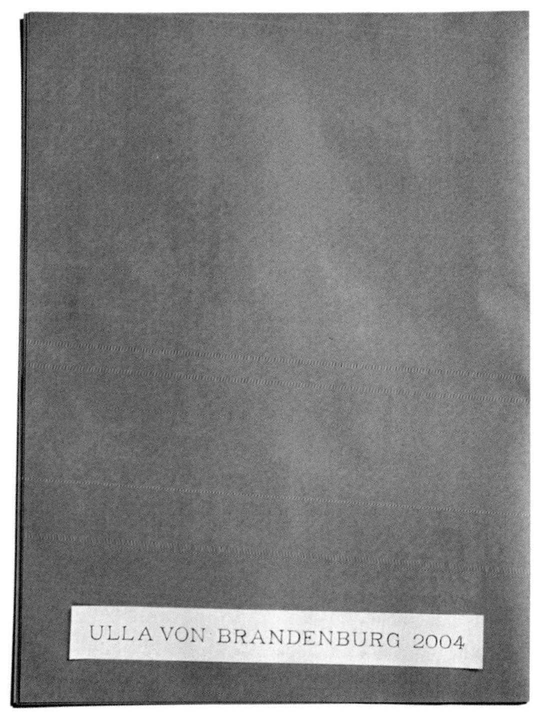
ULLA VON BRANDENBURG 2004

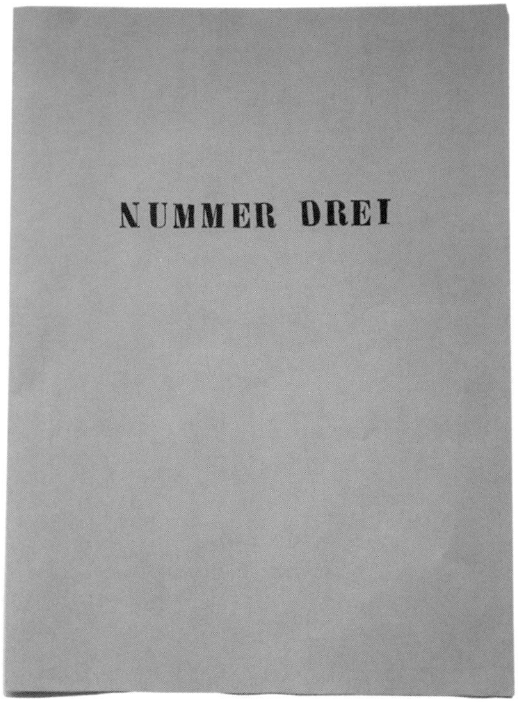

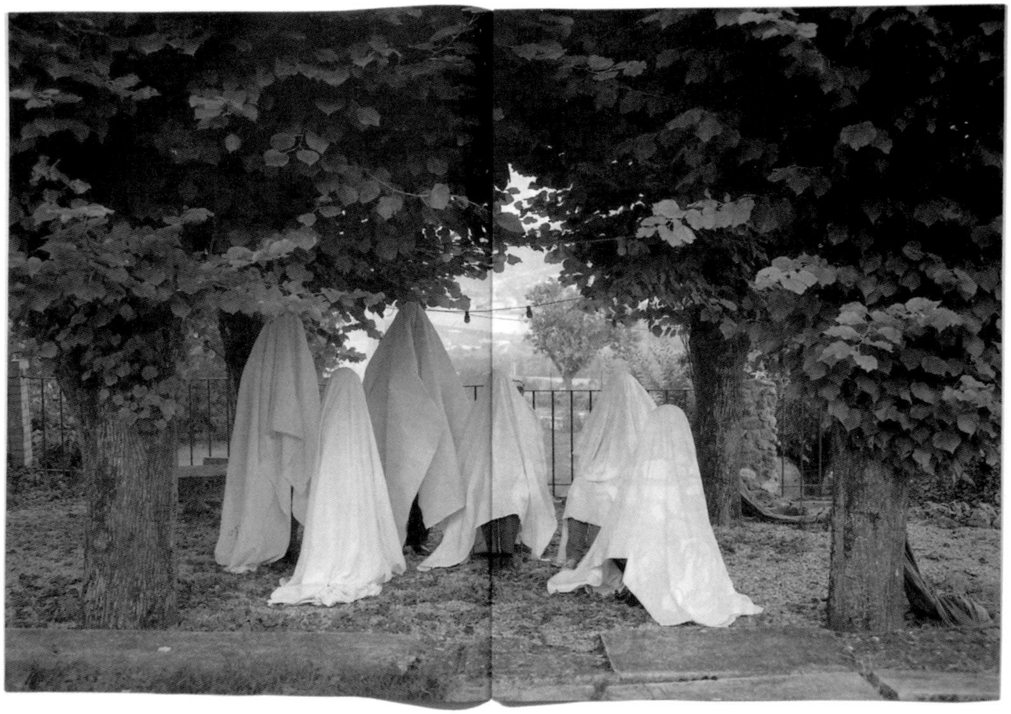

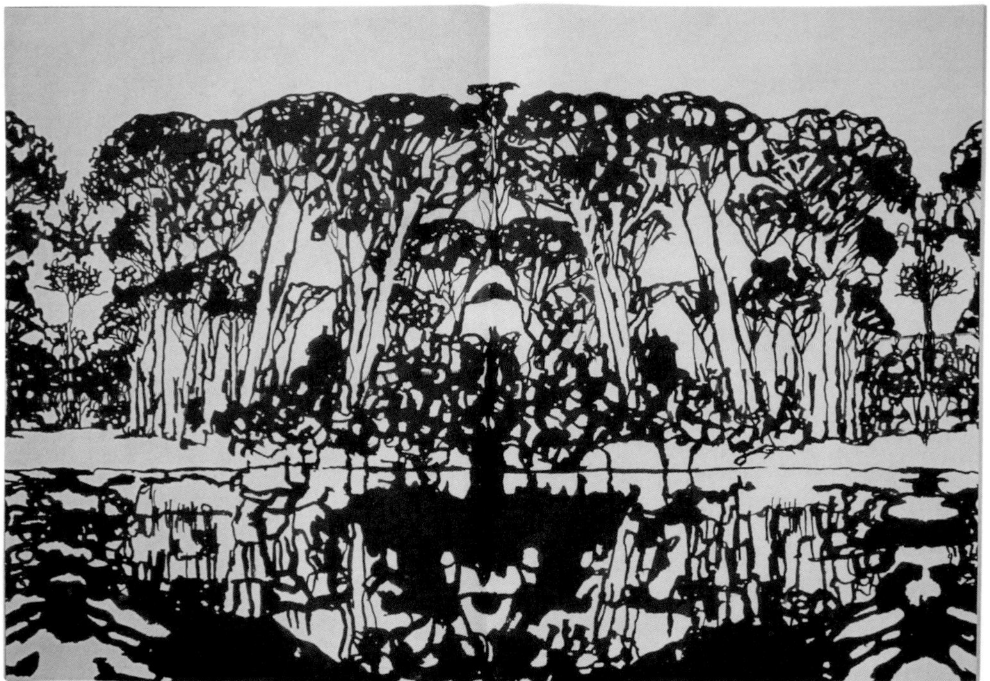

Nummer Drei (Number 3), 2006

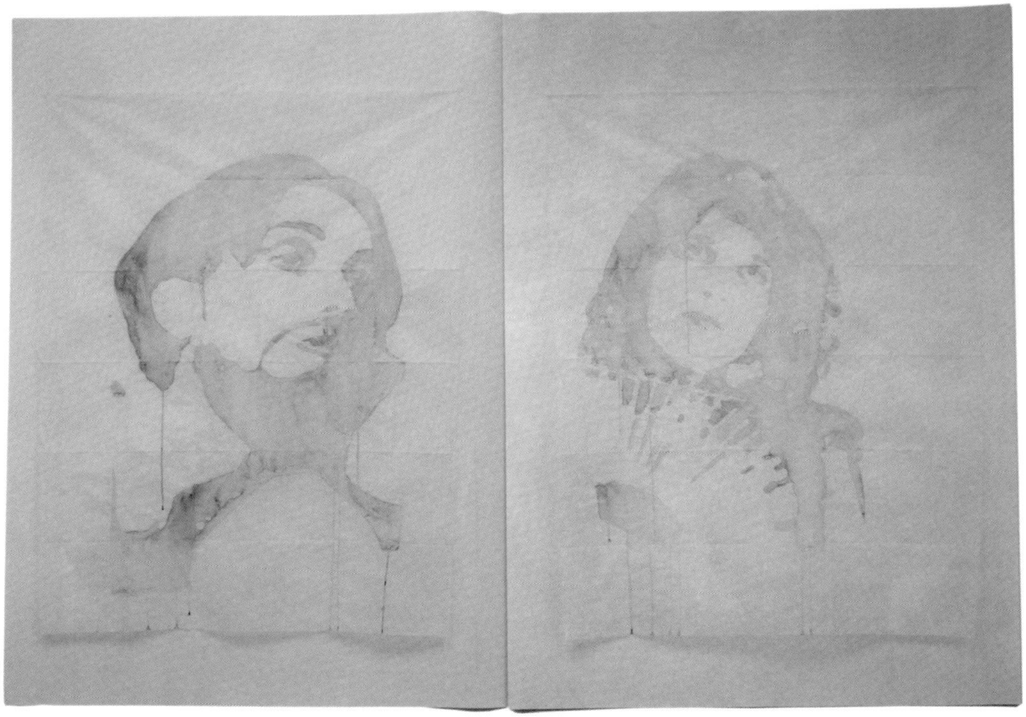

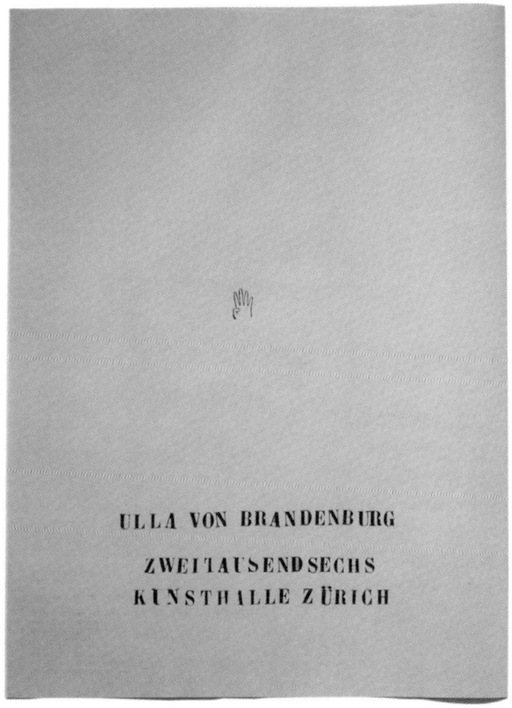

9 | Ulla von Brandenburg

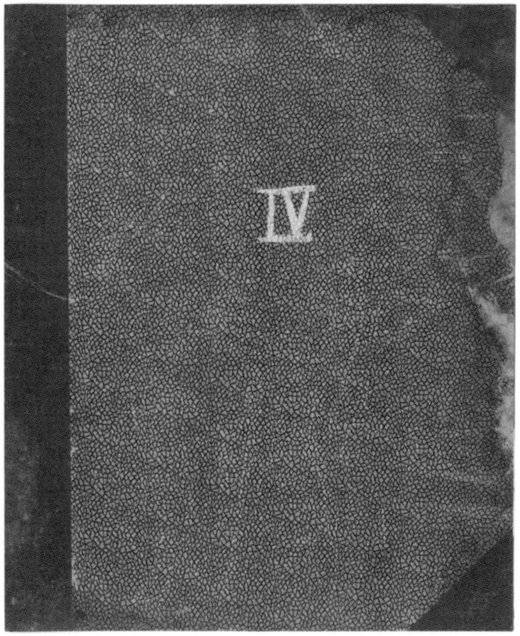

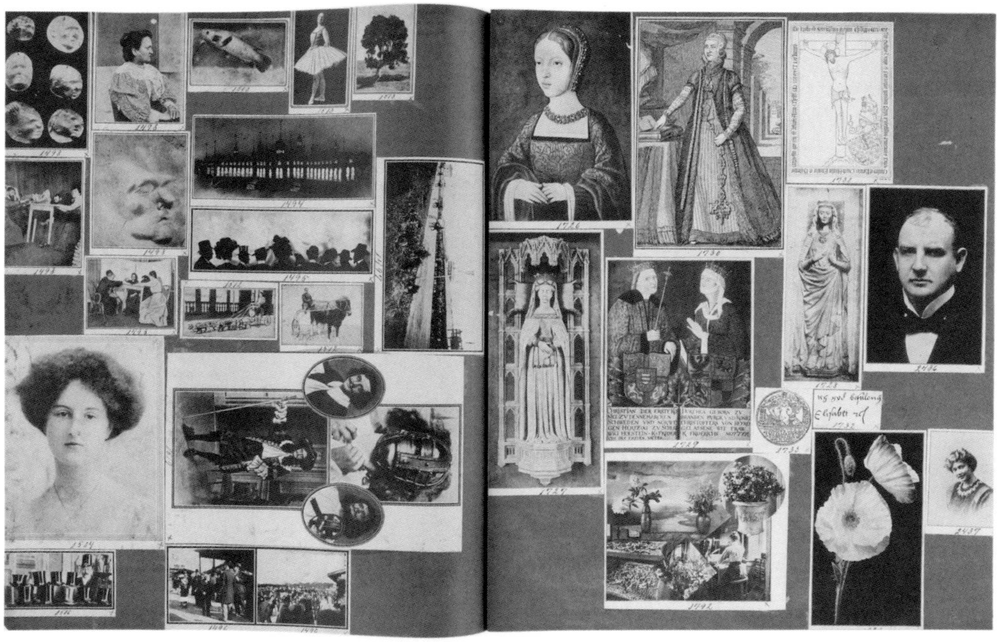

IV., 2008
Overleaf *Band (Ribbon)*, 2007

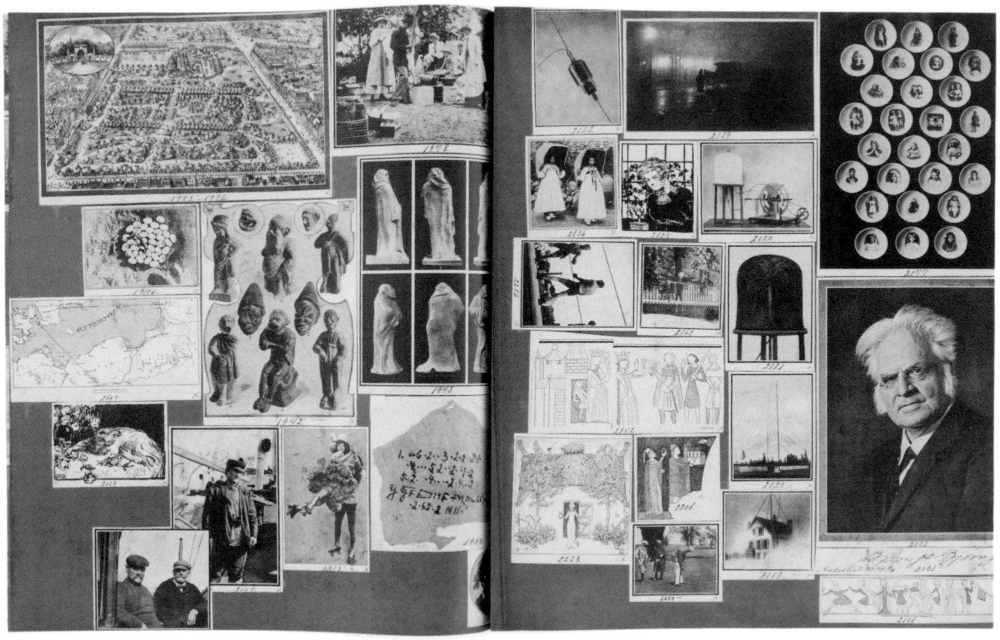

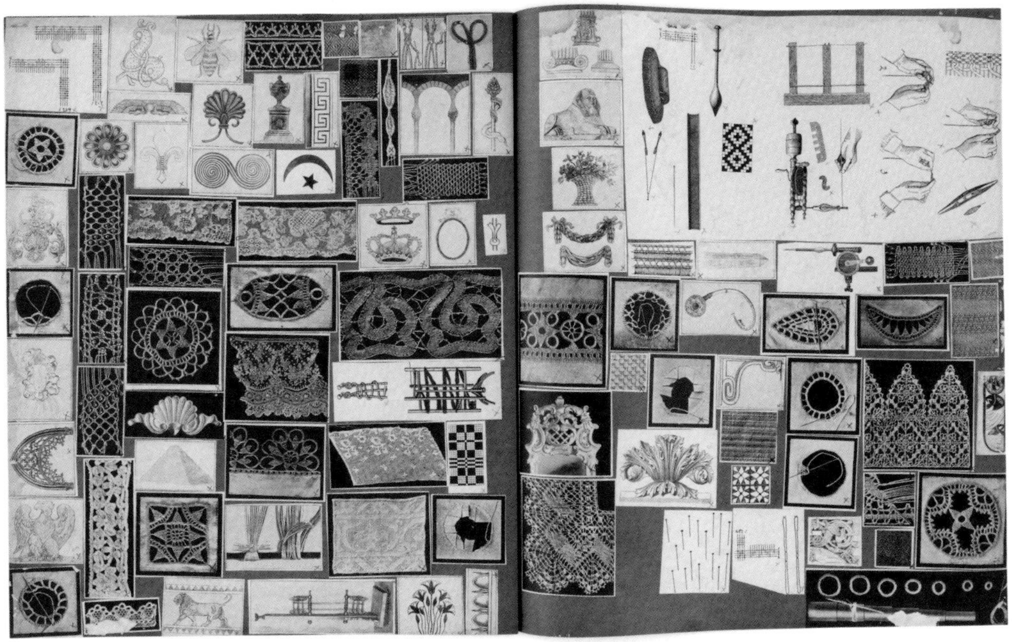

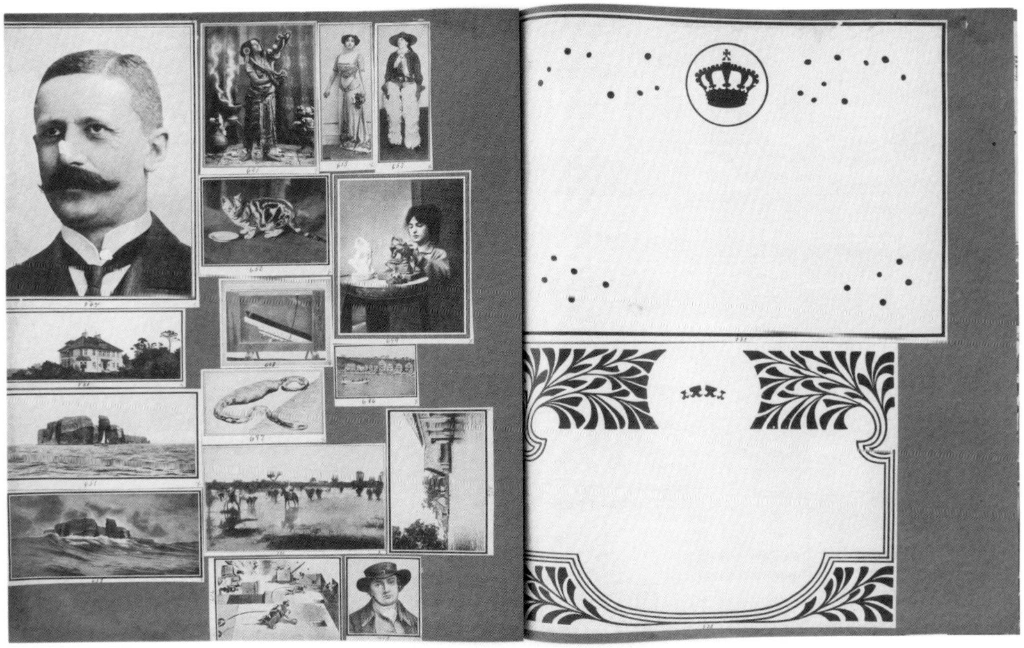

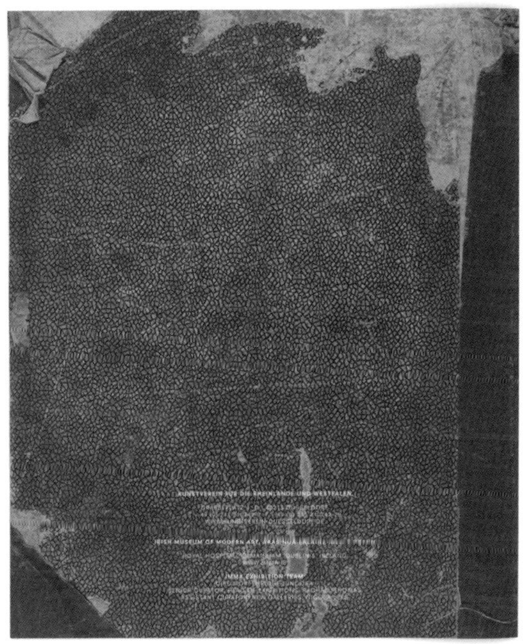

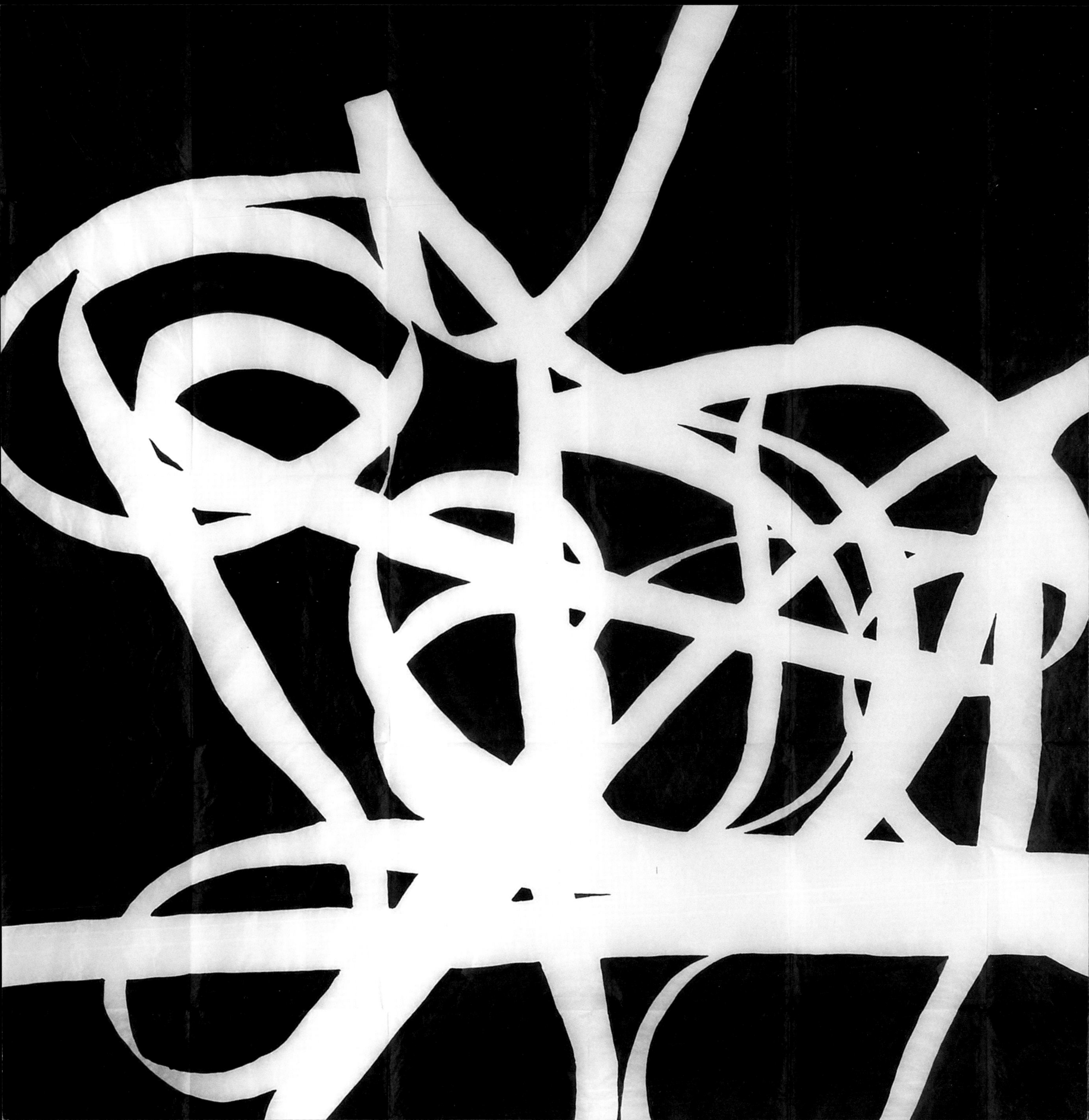

whose beginning is not, nor end cannot be

The following conversation between Ulla von Brandenburg and Rachael Thomas took place in the artist's Paris studio in March 2008.

RT
The title of the exhibition, '*whose beginning is not, nor end cannot be*', taken from the work *Angel-talks* by the great Elizabethan Magus John Dee, alludes to a number of related concepts that seem to be central concerns within your practice. An immediate association is the Renaissance Hermeticism idea that the ordering force of the universe is boundless, absolute, unknowable, multi-dimensional, and that any conception of order ormeaning which one finds in the world is illusionary. Existence has its own order and perhaps we are but shadows in its migratory stage-show. William Shakespeare draws upon this theme of illusion and life as theatre in his final play *The Tempest*, in which he modeled his central protagonist, Prospero, on John Dee. The play concludes with Prospero offering this insight into the radical insubstantiality of things:

> Our revels are now ended, these our actors,
> As I foretold you, were all spirits, and
> Are melted into air, into thin air;
> And, like the baseless fabric of this vision,
> The cloud-capp'd towers, the gorgeous palaces,
> The solemn temples, the great globe itself,
> Yea, all which it inherit, shall dissolve,
> And, like this insubstantial pageant faded,
> Leave not a rack behind. We are such stuff
> As dreams are made on; and our little life
> Is rounded with a sleep.
>
> (The Tempest, Act IV, Sc. 1)

Perhaps then you can begin this discussion by talking about the title of the exhibition and the associations it holds for you?

UB
This sentence is from '*A True and Faithful Relation of What Passed for Many Years Between Dr John Dee and Some Spirits*', also called the *Angel-talks*. Magus John Dee was a great mystic, but also a scientist. He wrote this text in 1659, when science was not separated from belief. I chose this sentence for the title of the exhibition because it is so dense that it can be taken to refer to so many different things and yet, it still has the energy of something whole and specific. Of course, the title refers to the nature of beginnings, both our own and the beginning of everything. And this introduces such a simple idea – if we never start or begin, then we would not exist. To me the phrase reads like a tautological rhyme. It suggests that everything we know about ourselves is inside. We see what we want to see and there is no reality, or, like Plato's allegory of the cave, illusions are our only reality. I am interested in exploring how the unconscious constructs reality. We all come from an eternal stream of unconsciousness, which signals to us in our dreams, while we are sleeping. As metaphysical beings, we are connected to water, fire, earth and air. These ideas relate to a performance I did entitled *Geist* (*Ghost*, 2005), in which there are three ghosts, three actors covered with sheets. The performance is an inverted séance; the ghosts would like to see a human being. One of the ghosts uncovers himself and sings a song about being alive, but then despairs and covers himself up again. You see, I am interested in the borders of different consciousnesses: past and present, alive and dead, and real and illusionary.

RT
If the world is rendered as theatre, as in *The Tempest*, the notion of performance takes on considerable importance. Significantly, there is a distinct staged and performative

quality in your work, such as *Curtain* (2007), and notably in your adaptation of the tableau vivant. How does the idea of staging and performance feed into your practice as a visual artist?

UB
There are so many aspects of theatre that I draw upon. The spoken literary language of theatre is both poetry and narration and it is immediately alive. So on one level, I'm interested in theatre as literature and how theatrical texts are written. But on another level, I'm interested in the theatre as a constructed space, like the traditional playhouse where you have the stage, the curtain and the audience. The curtain is somehow the borderline or the frontier between two worlds, which are mirror images of each other. It demarcates where reality ends and the illusion of life, feelings, emotions and events begin. So although you identify with the characters, and perceive their emotions as your own, you also create a distance because it is not real – it's a repeated replication. This duality is important in *Curtain*. The idea was to have this huge curtain hanging as people pass by so they don't know which side of it they are on. Are you on the side of the actors or the audience? Something similar occurs in Buñuel's film, *The Discreet Charm of the Bourgeoisie (Le Charme discret de la bourgeoisie)*, 1972, when a group of people are sitting around a table and then one wall, or what seems to be a wall, opens up and there are spectators there watching. The people sitting around the table are no longer subjects, but objects of the spectator's gaze. What I also find appealing about theatre or performance has to do with its immediacy, the live act of creating something out of nothing. It exists only while it is being performed and it is not preserved through documentation. It is ephemeral, like us.

RT
This notion of a narrative or a performance elapsing over time seems related to how you have constructed this exhibition at the Irish Museum of Modern Art. Can you talk us through the structure of the exhibition and describe how the different elements and the diverse variety of media used in your work, including film, painting, drawing and a wall installation specifically designed for IMMA, are linked together?

UB
Well, the exhibition is structured like four, or even five, different acts or chapters in a play or a book. The first thing you see is a theatre curtain installed on the facade leading into the exhibition space, which you must pass through to get inside, like an 'Overture' in the opera. The pattern of the curtain is the same as the backside of the tarot cards which I developed. In this sense, what is behind the curtain is like the image of a tarot card. Of course, every tarot card has a different, very personal meaning and can be read in different ways, just like everybody can find a different interpretation behind the curtain in the exhibition. After you cross the curtain, you come to a clump of newspaper magazines that I have made for the exhibition and they act like an archive of my collected images. These are free to be taken away so anyone can use or borrow from this specific chapter of my archive for whatever reasons they wish, whether to put up on their wall or to use as a starting point to develop their own ideas. The idea is that there is never a finished work, that objects or incidents become part of the continuum of experience without a fixed beginning or end. Beyond this, there are drawings attached to the wall that are related to those in the newspaper and also to the film footage and images in the later spaces of the exhibition. Leading off from here, there is a niche where the film *Geist* (2007) is showing. In the second space, there is a wall drawing covering all four walls of the room. Like a diorama or panoramic painting, the drawing encloses you, putting you in 'another world', which is here a forest by night. All of the space is very dark and black, you see only the long trunks of the trees. The idea is to

transpose inside for outside, and night for day. In the third room, you see the piece *Karo Sieben* (Seven of Diamonds, 2007). This is a chessboard made to give the illusion of perspective, and it acts like an empty stage, or a receptacle for the spectators' ideas of what could happen. Props such as two walking sticks and a ribbon function like props for your inner scenery. My new film *8* (2007) in which a moving camera glides through the dreamlike interior of a castle, occupies the last space. This castle has different rooms like the layout of the exhibition space, so the film is somehow an extension of what you have just been doing while walking through these different rooms. So, these exhibition spaces are like chapters and this approach is consistent with my working practice, whereby I'm using all these different medias, but always cross-referencing back and forth, developing a language that loops back on itself, that repeats and develops from recurring themes and images.

RT
Like motifs appearing, fading and re-emerging chapter after chapter. It is interesting then that the occult investigations of John Dee re-surfaced and provided the momentum at the end of the 19th century for a wide-spread engagement with occultism, mystics and magic, as this is the period of history referred to extensively in your practice. In your work you engage with that era's cultural forms – tableau vivant, developments in photography and early cinema – and those in particular born out of occult preoccupations – tarot cards, séances, magic rituals, mediumistic possession, the circus and the fairground – as if you are creating an imagery of that period's collective unconscious, identifying subterranean urges that possibly cast light on our own times. Is this true, and what is it about this period and its kind of counter cultural manifestations that has made it a preoccupation in your practice?

UB
The 19th century for me is the century when all was still open, before modernism began. New methods of experiencing the world, new methods of communicating, experiments in photography, and the birth of film – which was considered at the time as an 'illusion machine' because of its ability to transform reality – all gave rise to a sense of profound change. It was a time when people didn't know everything, when mysteries had a place. I think that you need mysteries, things you don't know and you don't understand. With the development of science and the discovery of the unconsciousness by Charcot and Freud and many others, this unconsciousness suddenly didn't belong to us any more, and since then, we have been researching it. And so, like you said, this uniquely modern moment created a desire for arcane metaphysical quests, a desire for the lost. People were more preoccupied with questioning ideas about belief and disbelief and solving the puzzle of human identity, ideas which disclosed the complicated and divided nature of individuality. It's as if you cannot believe what is on the surface. There are many layers underneath us and many generations stretching before us. They are all influencing us right now and we don't even know it.

RT
In this sense an interesting parallel can be made between your practice and that of Joan Jonas. I recently saw her multimedia installation, *The Shape, the Scent, the Feel of Things* (2004—2005), and was struck by how it revisits all these ideas about the American landscape and the psyche by layering and combining performance and shifting tableaux of tribal and occult imagery.

UB
Yes, like how she returns to past topics, images and ideas, reflecting upon diverse cultural sources until they become a system with their own dynamic. In this work, Jonas portrays her experiences as a child, the Hopi

traditions with the snake dance, and the journey of the art historian, Aby Warburg, to the American Southwest. She explores these influences through video projections, performance, spoken word, sound, and image in a stage-like space. Her visual vocabulary is like an open system, which she mixes up in many different ways, often directly accessing the unconscious. Also, I am interested in how Jonas re-uses segments of works that she has shown already, many years before, in a different context. These segments are reorganised to create new meanings. In Jonas's work, nothing is ever finished, or has an end. Each time a work is shown, the piece acquires a completely different meaning; as an artist, you are always changing, so when you re-use material from an older work, that material takes on a new relevance for you. Jonas creates complex worlds by weaving many layers from the past and present, and from mythology and history. She has said that she is interested in the process of collage, of putting one thing next to another to make something new, a third thing. It is this idea of using two already known things to create something unknown that I am interested in.

RT

The period at the end of the 19th century is characterized by many different velocities of movement. You mention developments in photography, the emergence of cinema, and these changes, along with advances in perception theory based on discoveries that the eye and nervous system are in a constant state of movement, all gave rise to an obsession with the nature of motion. What seems fascinating in your practice, particularly in your adaptation of the tableau vivant, is a provocation that stillness is about to break into movement. In a trilogy of works made in the 1990s, and including *Lapsus Exposure* (1992—94), *I N I T I A L S*, (1993—94) and *Background* (1991—94), the Irish artist, James Coleman, uses a slide projector and series of dissolving tableaux vivants to create tension between immobility and movement, which confers on the images a strange narrative atmosphere. Similarly, in your work, suspended action stimulates anticipation. Can you tell me about your use of the tableau vivant?

UB

The tradition of the tableau vivant existed as far back as Goethe's time – Goethe himself did them, it was a kind of fashion in those days – and even in the early days of photography, the long exposure times meant that subjects had to remain still, creating in effect, scenes like a tableau vivant. Yet photography fixes the moment in time, killing the vivant or life, and as a consequence, I became interested in the possibilities of filming tableau vivant, using mainly super 8 or a 16 mm black and white camera, to capture a sort of in-between time. So in these films you see all these characters as if in photographs, but you also see that they are blinking or straining to remain motionless for the duration of the work. Also these immobile performers in staged poses raise an issue around behavioural conventions. Do we construct how we act in everyday life according to theatrical images, societal rules or patterns observed in our parents? These static performances serve to deny individual identity or character – even the smallest movement gives away so much information about who you are, and I am interested in eliminating this. There is a similar idea behind my black and white drawings, which flatten pictorial depth, but generate a different spatial dimension into which ideas can be projected. In this way the figures and their positions within the image become more representational so that the position of the card player, or the Greek muse, function as symbols or archetypal poses that circulate across time. The original idea of tableau vivant was to restage already existing paintings, bringing them to life. This idea is drawn from the ancient Greek myth of Pygmalion, a sculptor who fell in love with his statue. In my film *8* there is only one real painting in the castle. From this painting, the camera moves to focus on characters from other paintings, which you can't see at this very moment. The people in the castle become substitutes for the paintings.

RT
An important process in this practice is taking specific historical source material and transforming it into the present. You do this for example in your filmed tableau vivant, *Kugel* (2007), *Der Brief* (2004), *Reiter* (2004), or by means of abstraction and shifting medium from photographs to painting in a work like your early wall drawing depicting a girl lying in a bed, *Untitled* (2003).

UB
Yes, it's re-contextualizing scenes or particular poses of historical origin to explore them as universal codes or behavioural rituals. Importantly, there is always narrative implied in these images. For example, *Kugel* is almost a Beckettian scene where people are waiting for something to happen, which could be a rehearsal for a play or the start of a strange Masonic-like ritual, but it never happens. And when you see these almost imperceptible movements you wonder if the actors are stuck in a situation that requires the impossibility of stasis. You sense that they are actually waiting for something to happen. So they are like staged rituals in a way. There is this scene in the film *8* where a father is lying on the bed and you don't know if he is ill or dying. And at the same time, as this is a staged theatre piece watched by an audience, there are sensations of anticipation and distancing.

RT
This work *8*, which is your latest film, signals a new direction away from static representation into filmic time, while simultaneously casting a backward glance at your earlier work. The film's narrative is created by a slow single tracking shot moving through a baroque French castle in which the camera is suddenly confronted by your previous tableaux vivants and other objects referring back to your past work. Can you tell me about this new shift in your work? Would you say it is a new direction?

UB
Yes. I think the new thing is that I am trying to connect a lot of the tableaux vivants with each other, and approach these earlier scenes in different ways. Equally important is the movement of the camera. This mobile viewpoint is both participating and observing. It becomes a personality moving between the tableaux vivants, drawing out networks of relations. It also introduces an additional spatial dimension, taking away the flatness and transfiguring the people and objects within. It brings to life a separate world that not only casts new perspectives on my previous work, but also dramatises narrative links between them. Again it is about the idea of repetition, and because the film is on a loop, it is always repeating itself. You don't see where the beginning is or the end. In fact, there is no beginning or end.

RT
The evocative ghostly presences in this film suggest a process of dissolving the parameters of the present and the co-existence of time past, present and future. Freud's account of the uncanny in his essay *Das Unheimliche* (1919) goes someway, I feel, towards elucidating the mood or atmosphere of the work. The uncanny, according to Freud, is often that which was once familiar being suddenly revealed, as when the spirits of the dead return to walk among us. How influential, if at all, is Freud's conception of the uncanny to your recent working practice?

UB
It's a very important concept and, like you said, the film is structured around the restoration of my previous tableaux vivants. But the concept has always been a presence in my work. From early on, I was interested in the idea of recycling images, evoking the obscured

familiarity of the strange, and this of course is evident in my latest work. For instance, there is an image of a woman with her hair covering the front of her face, which is a feature of my first film. And Freud's essay also talks about repetition, coincidence and uneasy encounters with oneself, like the sensation you have when you see somebody unfamiliar in the mirror and then a second later, you recognise that it's you. These are all aspects of the *Unheimliche*. It suggests that we have many different conscious or unconscious sides, or, you could even say, many different lives. It suggests that earlier experiences in our lives are still with us, a part of who we are, and that they are intent on coming out, telling their obscured tales. I find it very interesting to try and open up this field, to suggest that it is important to see all of these hidden faces in the mirror.

RT
The film *8* has been presented within a labyrinth-like structure made from coloured lengths of fabric. Interestingly, in the West, ideas about colour evolved out of alchemy and magic. For Goethe colours have primal affective characteristics. In his influential *Theory of Colours* (1810) he wrote 'Every colour produces a corresponding influence on the mind'. What effects are you aiming to create through the colour combinations in the installation, both within the labyrinth-like structure and in its relationship to the black and white film? Do you attribute occult physiological powers to colour?

UB
I am very interested in open psychological systems that posit a universal language of colour – the Max Luscher tests, for example, are fascinating studies in personality based on colour preferences. The sensations that colours give us have a strong effect on us but they are enigmatic and we do not understand them very well even though they influence our actions everyday at an unconscious level. For me, it is intriguing to use these psychological associations to activate emotions in the viewer and certainly such ideas were behind the conception of the coloured arrangement. The labyrinth is designed to imitate the architecture of the castle, which you then see in the film. By passing through the labyrinth first, you somehow enter the film's rhythm and its consciousness. You see these colours and feel these different things, which you bring with you inside. Then, when you sit down to watch the film, there is a sense of a physical interchange or transposition. You're no longer moving and you're watching the film, but what you did before with your body, you witness the re-enactment of that. You see the camera moving through the space just like you did moments earlier. Somehow, you were the black and white narration held in this construction and then it doubles back – you see the film and the content and you are the colourful outside architecture.

RT
Your work also suggests a strong interest in conflicting representations of women and frequently you adapt sourced images organized around the female figure in liminal states. The images you adapt tend to be from the end of the 19th century and it is significant that the emergence of Victorian Spiritualism and occultism, which we have talked about, was intimately bound up with the role of women. This fact was used by many to consolidate conventional Victorian attitudes of the female character as irrational and hysterical, yet the feminization of spirituality also gave women a symbolic power as mediators between this world and another world. Your work seems to engage with these ideas?

UB
This is true, and again it goes back to the question of why there emerged, at the moment modern culture was born, a popular engagement with mysticism and occultism. It shows that there is a part of our culture that is fearful of women. The ideals of modernity made it necessary

to explain away spiritual experiences as forms of emotional hysterical typical in female psychology, and because of that, women were often the mediums. It was easier to connect these unknown and 'otherworldly' symptoms to a woman than it was to a man. Yet I do not doubt that these conditions existed or escalated during this period. I mean if you look at the corsets women were expected to wear, they were an invention to create an hour-glass figure, but they also had the effect of impairing breathing, causing symptoms such as fainting that were attributed to hysteria. But for me, hysteria also became a means to rediscover the unconscious or connect with something outside that which surrounds us in this reality. I mean, it is almost dreamlike. Illness or hysteria was an escape for many women out of this very male organised society.

RT
It is a feature in the important plays of this period, such as August Strindberg's *Miss Julie* (1888) or Henrik Ibsen's *Hedda Gabler* (1890), that the dominant female character ends up committing suicide as a means of finally escaping the constrictive roles society demanded of her…

UB
Yes, and also these women did not have so many ways to explore their personal interiority, act out their desires, or have power in their society. However, Ibsen and Strindberg, and Edvard Munch too, were obviously afraid of the oncoming female emancipation movement at that time. They were afraid that women might gain the same powerful positions as men. They feared losing power, and therefore, many women in these plays or paintings have to die, go crazy, become mean or suck the energy from men. For me it is also interesting that these all became different forms of release. Hysteria, illness, or mediumship – they are ways to escape from the world. However, the most interesting thing to me is not investigating the qualities of femininity at this time, but rather understanding all of the things that symbolise either femininity or masculinity, and the ultimate 'constructedness' of being a woman or a man. In theatre, you have the potential to play with these qualities. You can have a man singing with a woman's voice, or woman wearing a man's costume, for example. In shifting sexual symbols in this way, you reveal gender as something that is performative. I am interested in all the customs we inherit, and the roles that we act out. On the stage, you have the opportunity to explore all of the many aspects that comprise a person, and that comprise people. Wearing costumes, for instance, can reveal a certain part of who you are. Performance then, is a process of psychological unraveling.

RT
Thank you, Ulla. For me, this talk has clarified the continuing sense of wonderment that is elegantly evident in you practice.

END

Tarot: Roy de Bâton (King of Sticks), 2008

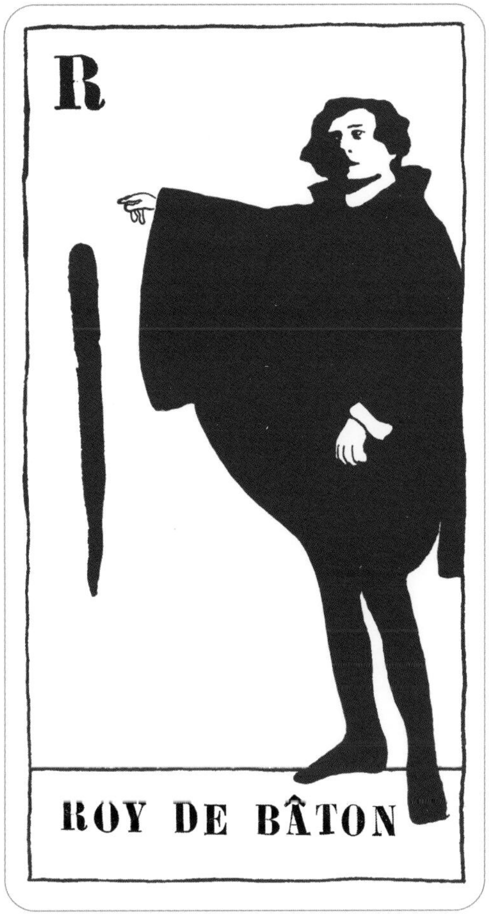

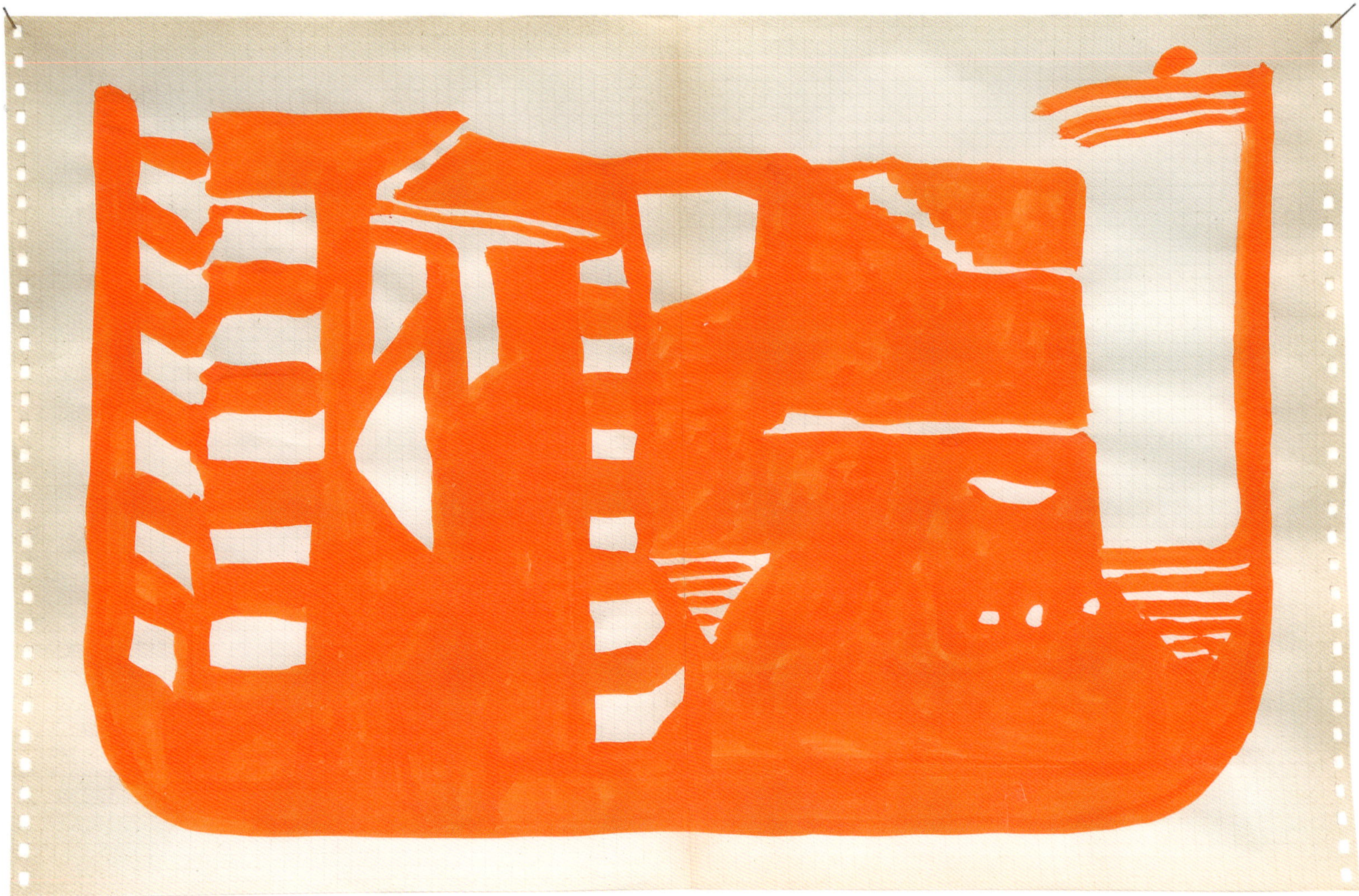

Bühne 1 (Stage 1), 2008

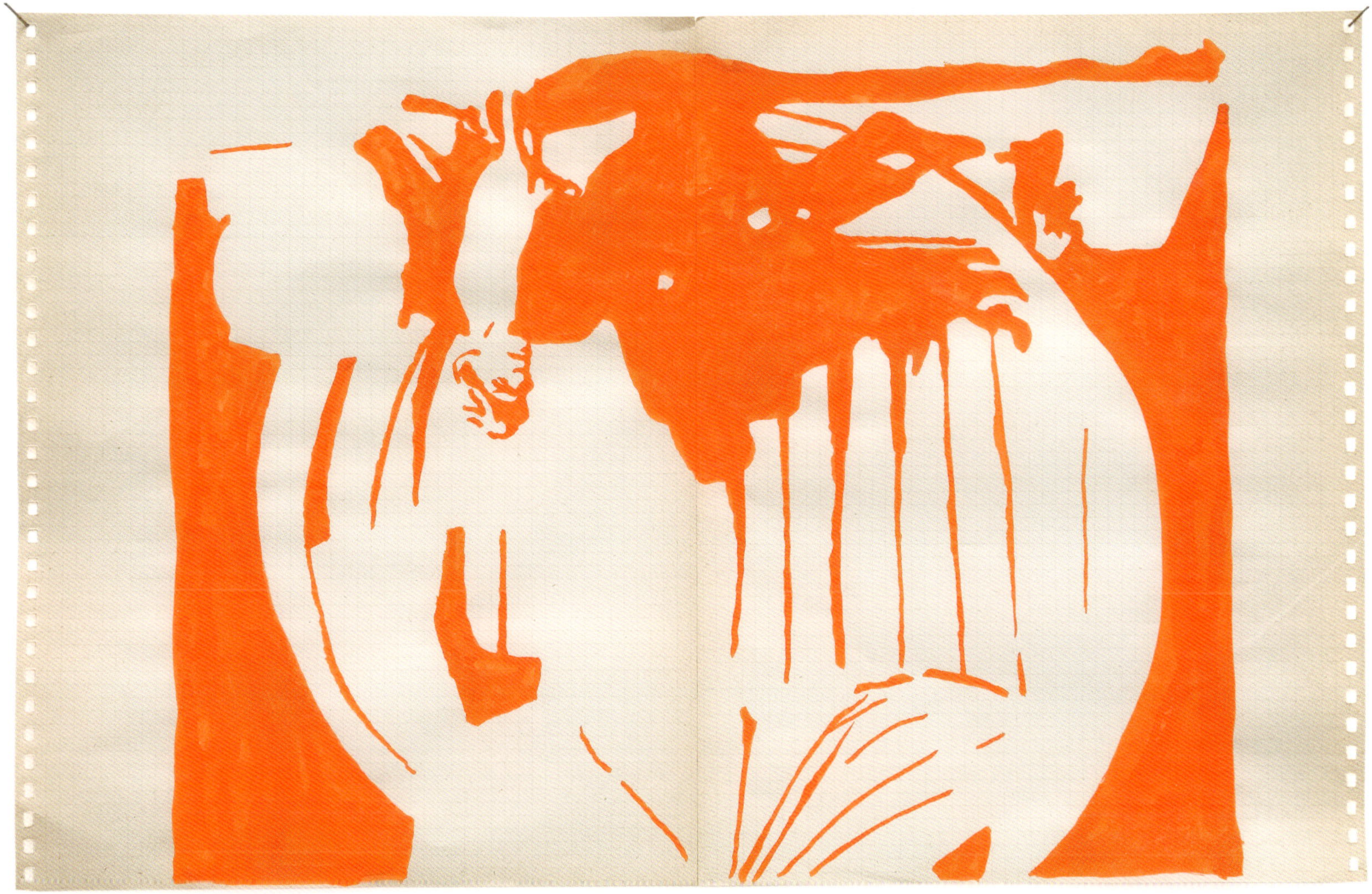

Bühne 2 (Stage 2), 2008

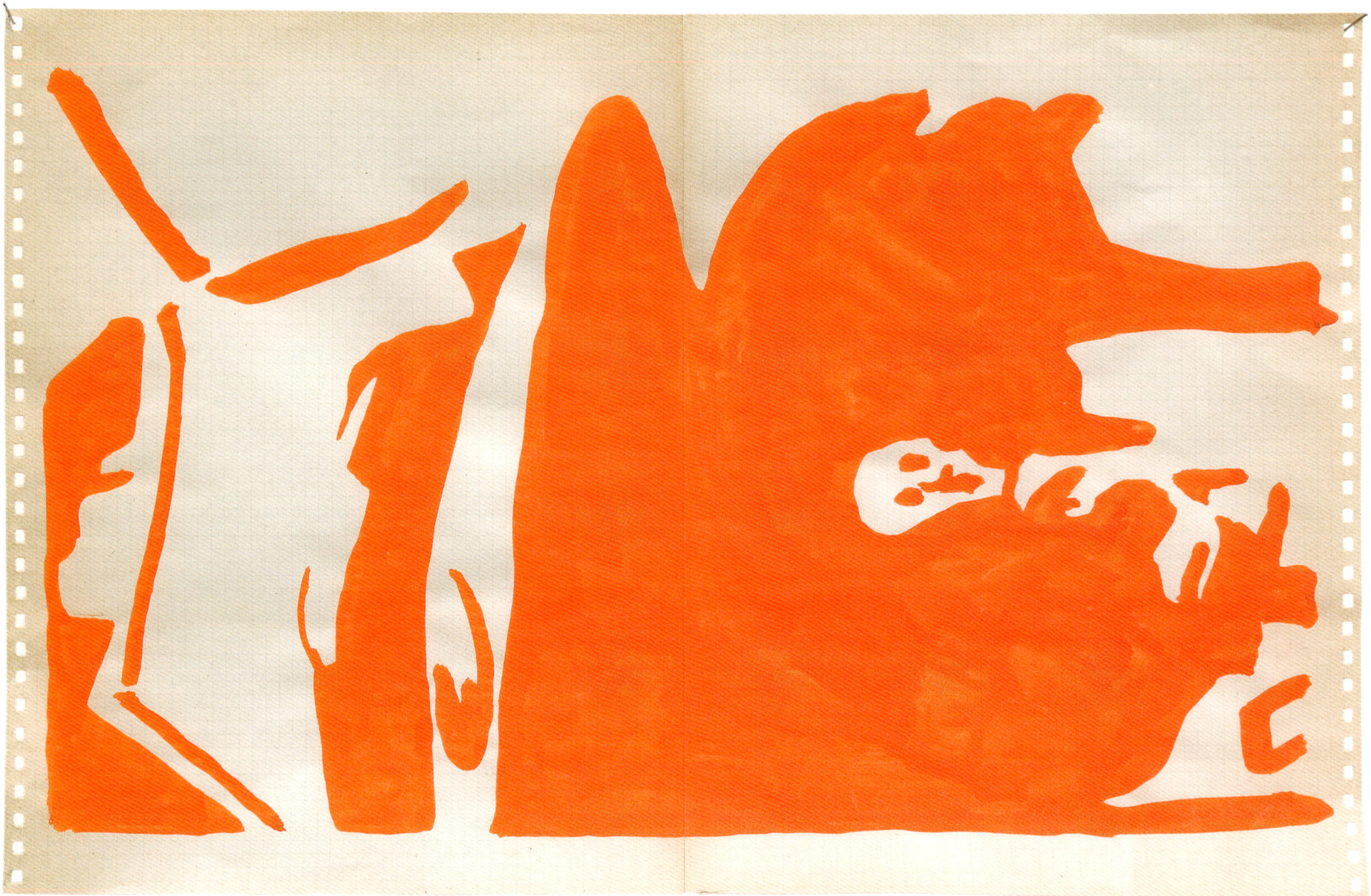

Kopf (Head), 2008

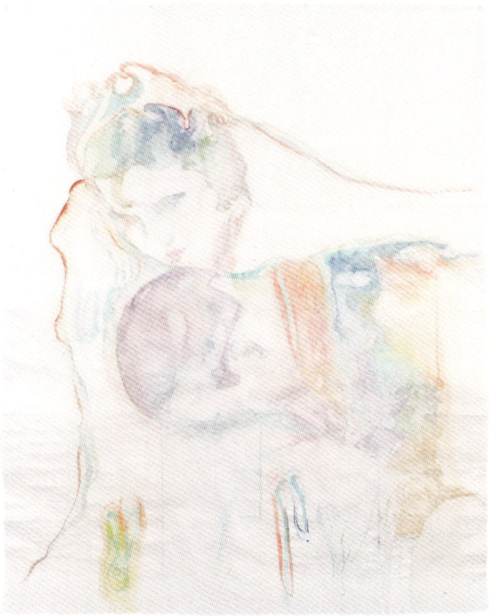
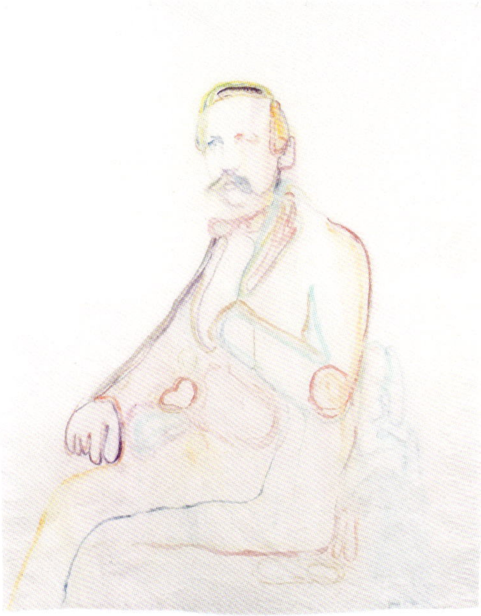
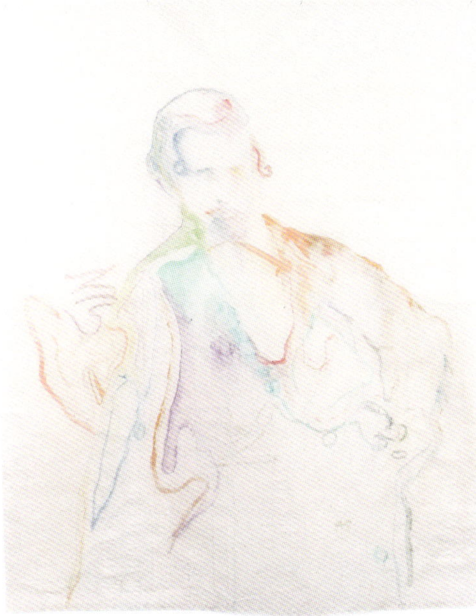
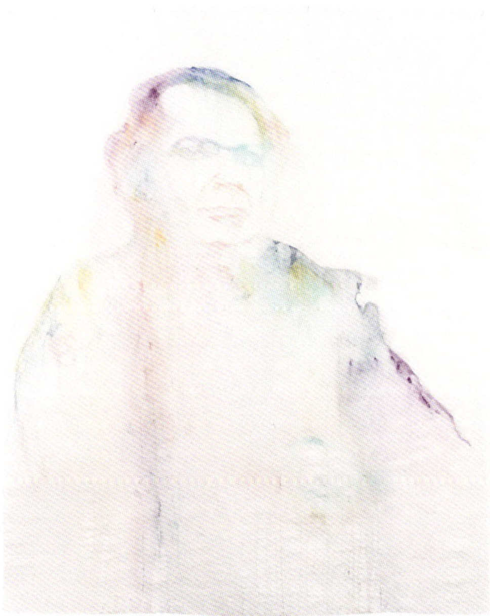
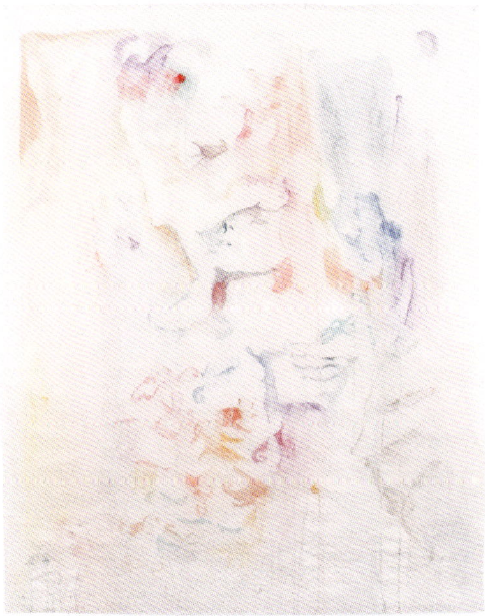

Spectre (Ghost) I—4, 2008

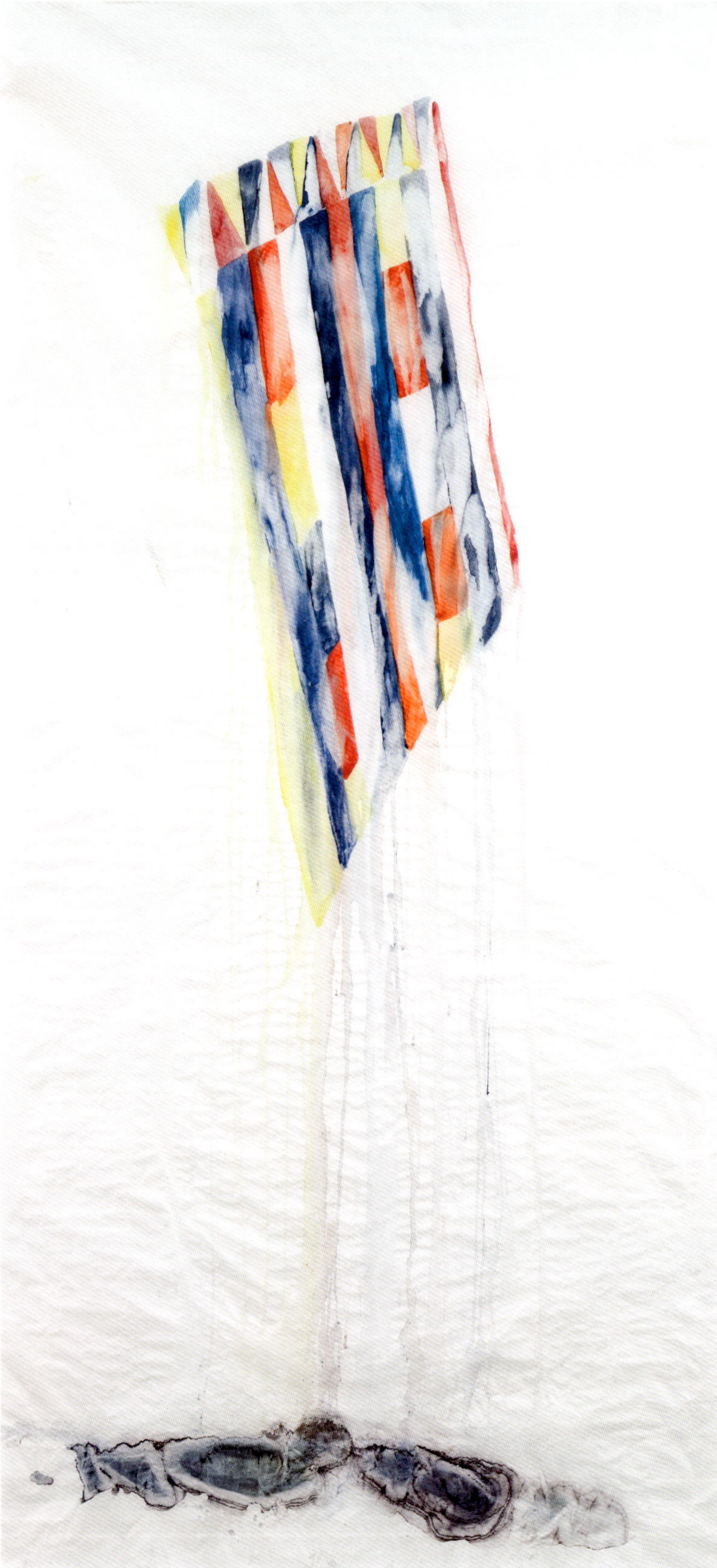

Segel (sail), 2008

Baender, Mann mit Tieren,
(Ribbons, Man with animals), 2006

Overleaf *Fächer (Fan)*, 2003

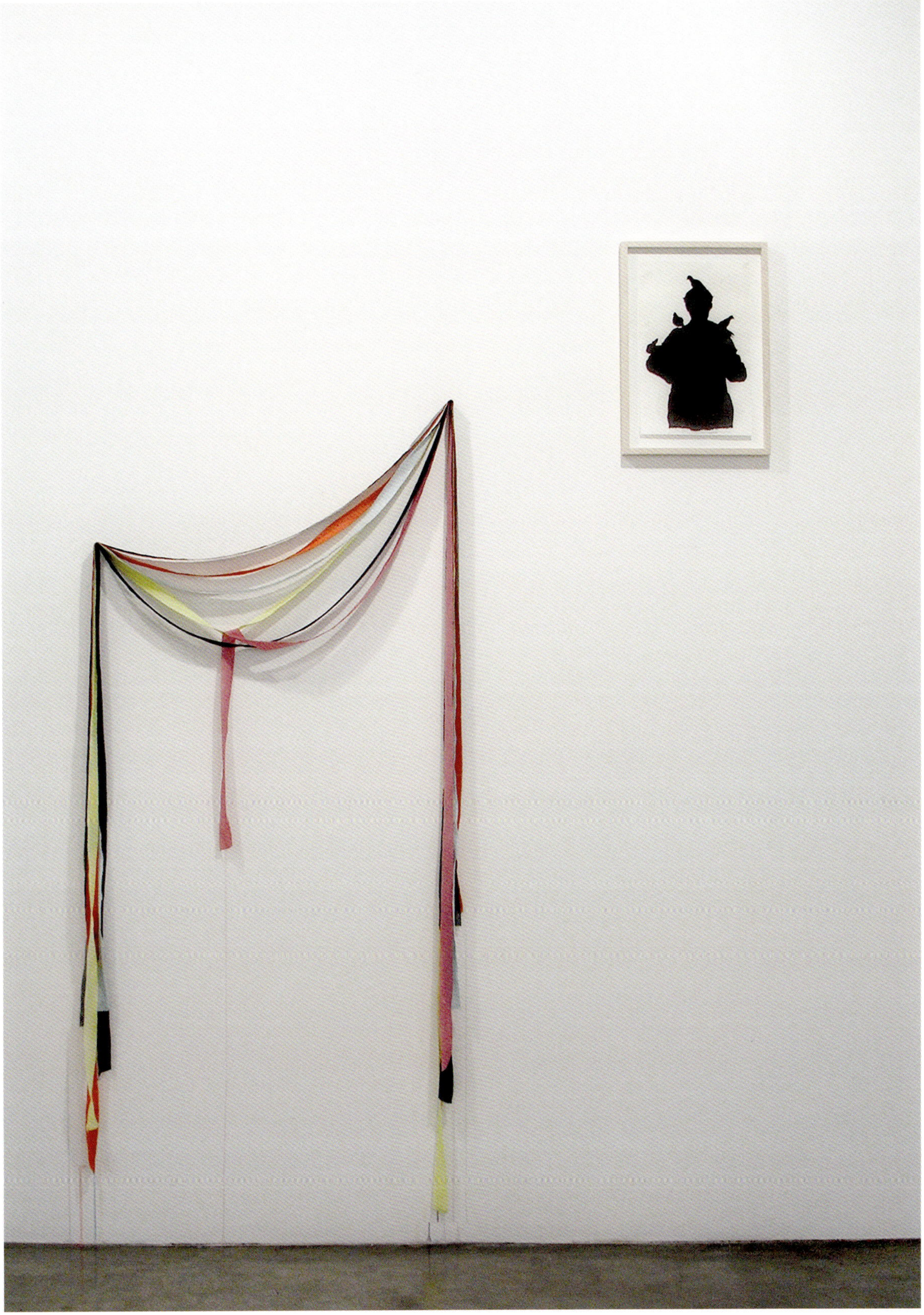

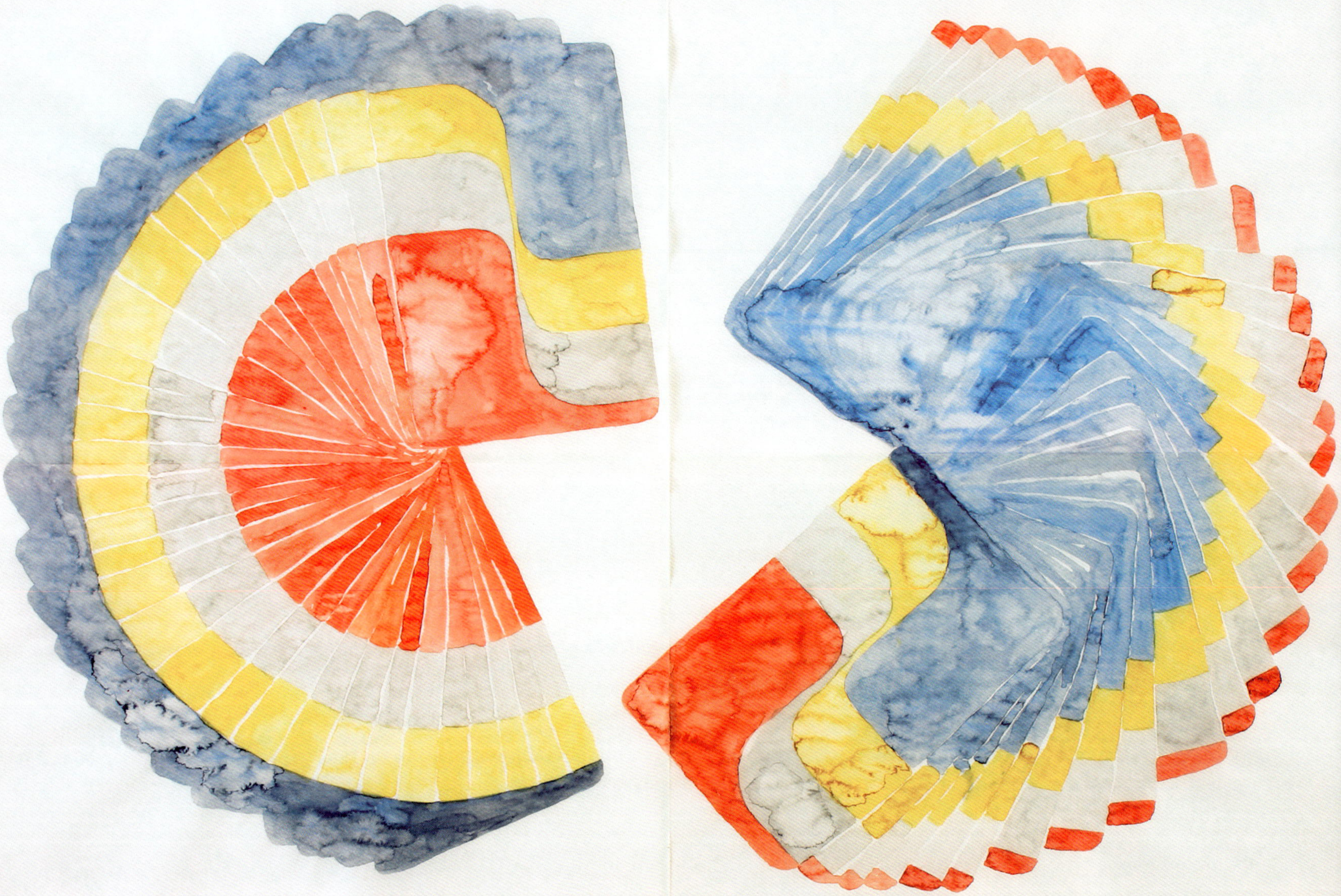

A Game of Worlds

Declan Long

It was not a dream… I was in a different state – I felt differently and strangely; and yet it was all as real, as clear and vivid, as what I now see and hear; it was a reality.
— J. Sheridan Le Fanu, 'The Familiar'[1]

He thought about the scene he had witnessed, how vivid it was for him, like an event he had observed before and knew well. He sat in his own armchair and allowed his mind to picture other rooms and doorways, other silent lockings of eyes and his own distant presence, as he read into the moment a deeply ambiguous meaning.
— Colm Tóibín, *The Master*[2]

I

At the beginning – if this is a beginning – there is the past. A serene river scene from a now-distant century: a still, hazy view of two men at leisure, casting fishing lines into the cool and steady flow of a country stream. The image is, we quickly learn, a fragment from a painted landscape, a simple glimpsed detail from an otherwise grandly theatrical vision of nature – here, curiously, captured by a hand-held camera with all the sensuous, antique-modern imperfections of black and white film. Several seconds pass before the lingering lens allows the full dreamlike splendour of the painted setting to be revealed – the humble human drama at the water's edge becoming quickly dwarfed by an imposing, stately architectural presence: a vast home abutting the river's far bank that seems to announce a triumphant ordering of nature's turbulence, a suspension of its temporality. In these initial moments from Ulla von Brandenburg's richly enigmatic film *8* (2007), we briefly contemplate a familiar bucolic version of nature: a staged, styled and preserved reality, a composed, contained idyll – the world brought to a perfect standstill. Yet, caught fleetingly as distancing monochrome film footage, the painting is emptied out of all ecstatic colour and confidence, stripped of all vibrant luminosity, all celebratory vividness. In these opening frames, we see a blurred and melancholy after-image of what may once have been imagined as an enduringly stable vision (and if, as the 18th-century garden designer Jean-Marie Morel once proposed, water is to the landscape as the soul is to the body, does it follow, then, that we vainly seek in the painting's central stream some trace of such necessary vitality?)[3] 'Life', should we wish to find it here, may be most surely evident in the ongoing movement of the camera's searching, subjective gaze – a speculation that recalls, perhaps, Pier Paolo Pasolini's wish to connect the sensory continuities of life with the 'long take' of cinema and to define death as 'lightning quick montage'.[4] But as the focus shifts away from an archaic, painterly idealization of the external world and we begin to progress through the elegantly austere, historically evocative interior in which the framed landscape hangs, a sense of ambiguity and uncertainty about this guiding cinematic 'animation' becomes slowly heightened. While embodied presence subtly reveals itself in the jerks and shivers of the occasionally unsteady camerawork – a quality of these scenes that is consistent with the appealingly calculated 'amateurism' found recurrently in von Brandenburg's work[5] – there is an equal and opposite sense of being an airily 'absent' observer in an increasingly unreal or uncanny environment – a place peopled, as we soon discover, by strange, seemingly flesh-and-blood figures, who somehow appear to us as inanimate forms, fixed in space and frozen in time.

So, as soon as we begin wandering in this mysterious space, in this indeterminate time, we come upon a lone woman, in plain, modern, everyday dress, lost in thought and impassively staring through the glass panes of a closed external door. As we draw closer, something unmistakably *wrong* can be detected in the way the woman holds out her partially gloved hands – there is, in the awkward pose, a manifest indication of unnaturally arrested motion, and our immediate and unsettling impression is that she has not merely entered a state of forlorn reflection, but succumbed to a condition of inexplicable stasis. Other still more cryptic and disturbing characters and scenarios continue to present themselves as we journey – in a tense, unignorable silence[6] – deeper into a warren of interlocking rooms. In a dramatic white entrance hall, a young, thin man dressed all in black stares intently at a horizontal figure-of-eight made from white fabric – a looping symbol of infinity – held taut between his two raised hands. Opposite him, across the repeated black and white of a tiled checkerboard floor (at the edge of which rests a vaguely sinister, symbolically resonant, pair of walking sticks), another motionless man casts a cold eye on his close-up reflection in a huge, room-doubling mirror.[7] Further on again, in the bright, far doorway of a dark adjacent chamber, a woman clasping a carnival mask seems to meet our gaze, but before we can fully approach, before we might begin to comprehend, our view veers towards a static seated couple, each holding a hand of playing cards. One of the two is subjecting the other's upturned palm to prolonged scrutiny, as if paused in an act of fortune-telling, leaving us uncertain, potentially, as to whether this stalled scene involves innocent gaming or occult divination – whether it is an agreeable contest between intimate opponents or a mystical effort to connect past, present and future worlds. As we circle around, sunlight from a solitary window seems to spray over, and even *through*, the couple; suddenly, and temporarily, they are materially insubstantial: they become spectral. It is a beautifully chilling minor moment, incidentally intensifying the atmospheric ambivalence of the shadow reality conjured by von Brandenburg.

Every inscrutable element we encounter here, every fascinating and seductively disquieting detail, tends to bring darkness and light, death and life, into unnerving proximity. Most acutely, we are conscious that the unmoving figures appear neither quite dead nor wholly alive: freakishly halted in the midst of often obscure actions, they seem unearthly, inhuman beings – but not, perhaps, *definitively* so. Some of the mounting unease inspired by these imaginary confrontations may have a psychic and social source in the inherited, still-widespread assumption in our largely secular Western culture that, as Marina Warner writes, 'the difference between life and death depends on an *animus* or *anima* imagined to lurk within embodied personality' – for all the sophistication of our philosophies, 'it is still difficult to turn one's back on the deep hinterland behind the principle of animation.'[8] But von Brandenburg's vision may well stir in us still deeper anxieties, suggesting more uncategorizable and undecidable states of being. There is a perplexing and troubling in-betweenness to the esoteric realms envisaged in her complex, abundantly allusive works, and to the 'petrifying' world of the film *8* in particular (or '∞' as we should also think of it, given its unceasing cinematic motion, its Möbius band form). With its poised, trapped *dramatis personae*, its populated but simultaneously vacant spaces, its concurrently bounded and boundless sense of time, its 'normal' contemporary stylings and its paranormal allusions, this filmic fantasy might be characterized, like the numerous other *tableaux vivants* staged in von Brandenburg's absorbing *œuvre*, by a kind of unyielding ontological hesitation. The film brings us to a purgatorial place: we are caught between worlds. At one telling point, as we creep fearfully through a sombre, oppressive ante-room, we pass a besuited man, stiffly reclining on a hall chair, his face covered by a dark silky cloth. He is arguably the most deathly and frightening figure yet to feature here (a fugitive, feasibly, from one of David Lynch's imaginative labyrinths), but he is also the most verifiably *alive*: his deep, heavy breathing steadily evident beneath the obscuring shroud. The gloomy liminal location, the man's masked anonymity, the rigid pose: these might be enough to provoke trepidation, but, for this viewer at least, it is the addition of the silent breathing that truly, irrationally, inspires a muted terror – what might be the most 'natural' element in this weird combination having the capacity to rupture our sense of a rational reality, to (paradoxically) give a sense of 'the immanence of death in life'.[9] As Marina Warner has noted, the Latin terms from which we take our understandings of human animation ('animus' and 'anima') are dependent on the 'metaphor of breath, principle token of living being', but 'breath' in this way becomes unavoidably ambiguous: it is the essential material process of our biology, and yet, in our ever-slippery language, it also takes us via the verb 'spirare' ('to breathe'), to the always-troubling term 'spirit' – a form of 'breath' that may, metaphorically, have valid secular use, but that signals, in other chimerical super-natural belief systems, a world of lasting life in death.[10]

2

How strange it is to think of such ideas, to contemplate such images as those found in von Brandenburg's art, within the interconnecting rooms of the historic Royal Hospital Kilmainham, the 17th-century building that is home to the Irish Museum of Modern Art. How curious it is, in one regard, that the obsolete forms, arcane ideas and occult themes studied by von Brandenburg continue to bewitch and trouble us so thoroughly today – and how eerily resonant they therefore seem in the context of an institutional environment dedicated, in the most general sense, to treasuring (and, of course, testing) the cultural achievements of modernity. How oddly appropriate, in so many ways, von Brandenburg's interests and works of art are to this setting. As curator Jessica Morgan has written, this artist 'sees her surroundings through the filter or ghostly presence' of the historical tropes she chooses, 'as if our own time's uncertainties summon the appearance of an earlier manifestation of doubt' – and such strategies and intuitions seem so serendipitously suited to a museum location that cannot avoid maintaining, in its synthesis of external classical 'form' with interior contemporary 'content', a dialogue between 'our time' and earlier eras.[11] Indeed, it is tempting, perhaps, to forcibly link the uncertain states of suspended animation staged in von Brandenburg's films (and suggested too in her many wall drawings and fragile works on paper) with the specific, fundamentally 'remote' form of life once associated with these buildings: for as a military retirement home throughout almost three centuries, the atmosphere of the Royal Hospital must have been one of rarified, orderly distance from the brutal, enervating real world, its ageing denizens living out their last years in a place apart, existing in a disciplined dream-world at the distant edge of the city. The novelist Colm Tóibín catches some of this elevated otherworldliness as he imagines his literary ancestor Henry James arriving as a guest to the Royal Hospital in 1895, following an upsetting journey through poverty-assaulted Dublin streets:

> He was relieved as the carriage made its way up the avenue of the Royal Hospital, and surprised at the stateliness of the building, the sense of grace and symmetry and decorum in the grounds. It was, he smiled to himself at the thought, like entering the kingdom of heaven after a rough ride through the lower depths. Even the staff who came to greet him and take his luggage appeared different, of a heavenly disposition.

The 'palpable present-*intimate*'[13] – in a life full of failed intimacies – was, for James, the primary, sought-after substance of the novelist's universe; so it is intriguing to observe the small ways in which Tóibín seeks to register the elusiveness of this realist prize: introducing symbolism that invokes preternatural possibility, signalling unresolvable tensions (between tormenting, disordered reality and its ordered representation; between, once again, darkness and light), and, in other low-key moments, stressing quotidian mystery, the ghostly unknowability of the everyday.[14]

Repeatedly, during his short stay at the Royal Hospital, James is pictured gazing through windows or doorways, surveying at an anxious distance the lulling but bewildering world-out-of-time in which he is temporarily situated: these are literary images of reflective, fraught stillness that purposefully blur any notional line between inner and outer worlds – Tóibín implicitly reminding us of the challenges faced by writers of fiction, and by all artists, at that time of radically transforming conceptions of consciousness, hinting at the interpretative hunger of the modern(ist) era. Such shifts, of course, led to (and responded to) profound crises in belief, spawning widespread *fin de siècle* fascinations in putative alternatives to rational materialist means of deciphering the world: the type of occultist experimentation that held, for instance, W.B. Yeats spellbound from a young age (valued statesman; Ireland's finest poet; the founder of its national theatre; and he was, as W.H. Auden said, 'silly like us').[15] For the cultural historian Terence Brown, however, Yeats's undying commitment to spiritualist creeds also has an element of inevitability to it, when seen from a particularly Irish point of view. Ireland's folklore, with its 'hauntings, revenants and changelings', was, Brown argues, an 'integral part of everyday awareness, even in the middle-class world of Yeats's childhood', suggesting to a significant extent that 'there is something characteristic, even traditional, about his Irish instinct for the spooky and the domestic supernatural.'[16] Yet if there is a type of 'tradition' here, it is one formed and malformed – as all traditions are – in conflict with the forces of modernity:

> What seems like an innate Gothicism in the Ascendancy caste's preoccupation with dynasties, misalliance, ancestral houses – repeated motifs in their nineteenth century fictions – meant as well that spectral matters were never far from a social consciousness that anticipated, but feared it could not prevent, imminent ruin. The uncanny and the weird often broke through the surface of polite Irish convention, as spiritualist obsessions, and like the prevailing hypochondrias, found ready soil as the political unconscious maybe sensed seismic, threatening shifts.[17]

All of which might bring us back in the end – if this is an end – to our ontologically insecure surroundings in the 'palpable' present, to the theatrical confusions of inner and outer realities that characterize the *mises-en-scène* imagined by Ulla von Brandenburg, to the moment, maybe, when our disconcerting tour of the rooms and corridors in the film *8* takes us finally, once again, to that already forgotten landscape painting, to its unnaturally becalmed gardens and its opulent, but now uncannily alienating, architectural centrepiece. (Can this be an image of the home we have wandered through? Are we 'where we are not?')[18] Or, we could be brought, here and now, to one of the hushed, venerable, old interiors of the former Royal Hospital that now survives as a contemporary gallery, where the artist has chosen to turn space inside-out, or rather outside-in, depicting in a hazy, grandly incomplete drawing, elements of this building's expansive, cultivated environs – lightly exceeding architectural limits by presenting within these walls an impossible panorama, but one that is carefully, arrestingly, inexact: a version of the visible real that is little more than a spectral outline. Or, again, we may find ourselves encountering another rare and not-quite identifiable species of space (to borrow Georges Perec's time-worn phrase) such as that created in *Karo Sieben* (Seven of Diamonds, 2007): a gracefully minimal installation that suggests, in all its studied enchanted reticence, much that seems important about von Brandenburg's beguiling world. Across the floor, filling the room, is a field of checkered fabric: a giant perspectivally disorientating and mutedly multi-coloured cloth 'chess-board', onto which it is tempting (but inappropriate) to step – so drawing us towards a game in which we would neither have control, nor know which specific role we might play. And yet is this merely the set-up of a game? Isn't there also, hidden somewhere in the depths of history, an occultist connection to such checked mosaic floor patterns – Masonic connotations, deriving from the everlasting symbolic conflict between darkness and light? But any conceptual or historical grasp of this ambiguous grid will not be enough. For against the walls, two slender sculptural objects are also positioned. One is a black rope, tied as a figure of eight, but one that is loosening, extending – an unfinished, unravelling 'infinity'. The other is a pair of walking sticks, identical to those caught in our peripheral vision in *8*: two functional, everyday items that together take on a charge of menacing arcane meaning. In each case, there is a continual accretion of possible associations and a simultaneous stripping away of certainty. The 'chess-board' becomes, as it did for Vladimir Nabokov, a 'magnetic field, a system of stresses and abysses, a starry firmament', and it is likely that we will be both lost and trapped here.[19] Interpretatively 'pinned', seized in a state of worrying reverie, we become transformed into more of von Brandenburg's frozen players – held in state of troubled arrest, calculating our next move.

1 J. Sheridan Le Fanu, 'The Familiar', *In a Glass Darkly* (Ware: Wordsworth Classics, 1995), p.62.
2 Colm Tóibín, *The Master* (London: Picador, 2004), p. 34.
3 See Jean Marie Morel, *Théorie des jardins* (Paris: Pissot, 1776) The painting observed in the film is by Hubert Robert who in fact worked on many garden designs with Morel. It seems important to note that the stream in this image was not a feature of the original landscape — so perhaps suggesting, as Ulla von Brandenberg has speculated, that ideas of 'soul' have always been 'projections'. (In an email from the artist, 12/04/08)
4 Pier Paolo Pasolini, 'Observations on the long take', in David Campany (ed.) *The Cinematic* ed. David Campany (London & Cambridge, MT: Whitechapel Gallery &MIT Press, 2007), p. 86. Originally published in English (trans. Norman Macafee & Craig Owens) in *October*, no. 13 (Cambridge, Massachusetts: MIT Press, Summer 1980), pp. 3–6.
5 Kirsty Bell has noted that in von Brandenburg's films "there is none of the slick *trompe-l'œil* sometimes associated with tableaux vivants ... rather, [her] work displays an endearingly amateur quality that reflects both her early theatrical education in Karlsruhe and an active engagement with her community (the performers are almost all artists)". See Kirsty Bell, 'Ulla von Brandenburg', in *frieze*, Issue 106, (April 2007), p. 133.
6 I am thinking in passing here of lines from Philip Larkin's 'Church Going': "Once I am sure there's nothing going on / I step inside, letting the door thud shut. / Another church: matting, seats, and stone, / and little books; sprawlings of floors, cut / for Sunday, brownish now; some brass and stuff / Up at the holy end; the small neat organ; / and a tense, musty, unignorable silence, / Brewed God knows how long...". See the *Collected Poems* (London: Faber & Faber, 1988), p. 97.
7 'Cast a cold eye / On life, on death. / Horseman, pass by!', from *W.B. Yeats*, 'Under Ben Bulben', in A. Norman Jeffares (ed.), Yeats's Poems ed. A. Norman Jeffares, (London: Macmillan, 1989), p. 452.
8 Marina Warner, *Phantasmagoria* (Oxford: OUP, 2006), p. 9.
9 Hal Foster, *Convulsive Beauty* (Cambridge, MT: MIT Press, 1993), p. 21. Foster here develops psychoanalytical implications of the Surrealists' interest in a confusion of the animate and the inanimate.
10 Warner, *Phantasmagoria*, pp. 61—62.
11 Jessica Morgan, 'Ulla von Brandenburg', *Artforum*, Summer 2006, p. 338.
12 Tóibín, *The Master*, p. 26.
13 Henry James in a letter to Sarah Orne Jewett, 5 October 1901. Quoted in James Wood, *How Fiction Works* (London: Jonathan Cape, 2008), p. 29.
14 We might note during the Royal Hospital sequences such passages as the following: 'His room looked away from the hospital towards the river and the park. In the morning, when he woke early, there was a white mist over the lawns. He slept again, this time deeply and peacefully, and was woken by a tip-toeing presence in the room, moving in the shadows.' (p. 27). Or, elsewhere: 'He realized now that this was something he had described in his books over and over, figures seen from a window or a doorway, a small gesture standing for a much larger relationship, something hidden suddenly revealed. He had written it, but just now he had seen it come alive, and yet he was not sure what it meant...' (p.34). Or this exchange: '"You look like you've seen a ghost sir". "It's the living I've been looking at", he said' (p.38).
15 W.H. Auden, 'In memory of W.B. Yeats', in *Collected Shorter Poems* (London: Faber & Faber, 1966), pp.141—13.
16 Terence Brown, *The Life of W.B. Yeats* (Dublin: Gill &Macmillan, 1999), p. 38.
17 Ibid.
18 'For we are where we are not', Pierre-Jean Jouve, *Lyrique*, p. 59 quoted at the opening of 'The dialectics of inside and outside', chapter nine of Gaston Bachelard's The Poetics of Space (Boston, MA: Beacon Press, 1969), p. 211.
19 Vladimir Nabokov, *Speak Memory* (London: Penguin Classics, 2000), pp.223—4. The phrase 'a game of worlds', which provides the title for this essay is also taken from Nabokov. It appears in line 819 of the long poem 'Pale Fire' that is at the centre of the eponymous novel. (London: Penguin, 1973), p. 53.

Tarot: 6 de Bâton (6 of Sticks), 2008
Overleaf *Forest*, 2008

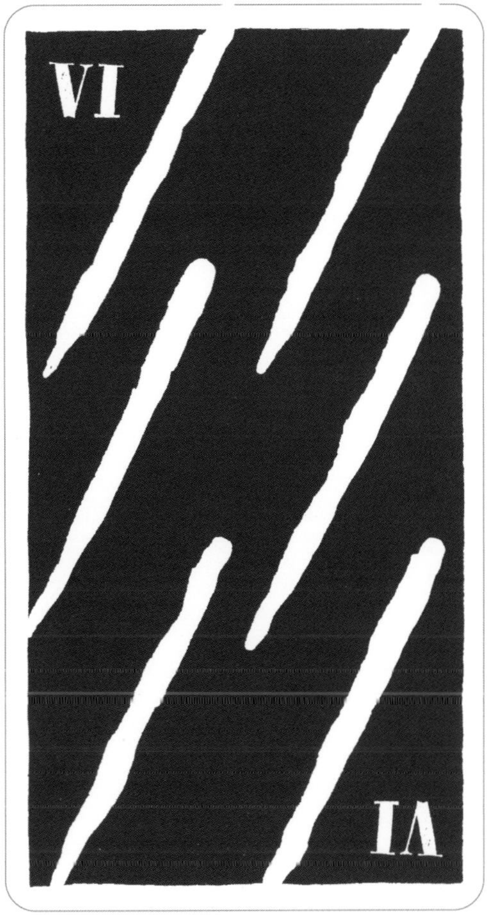

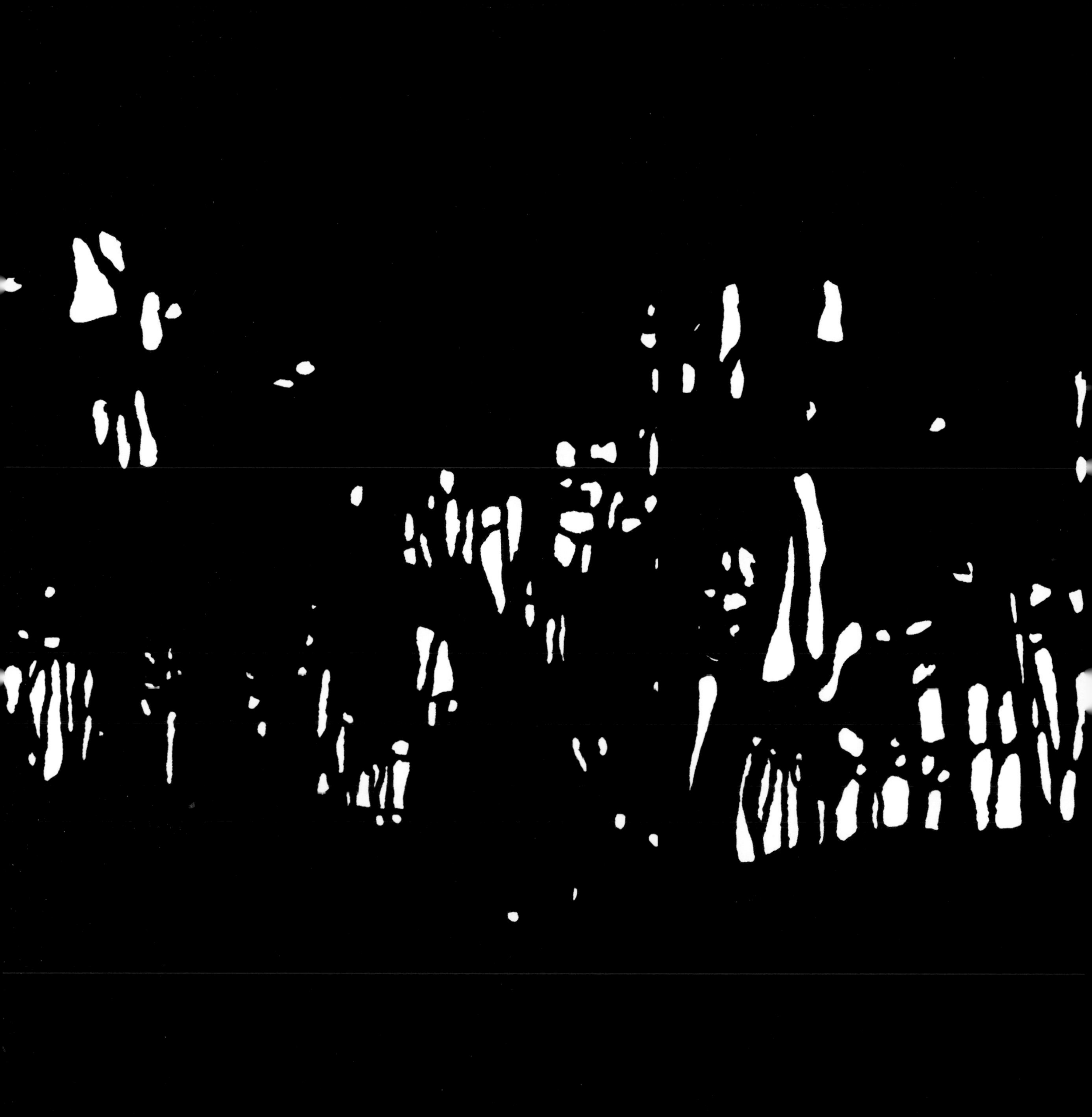

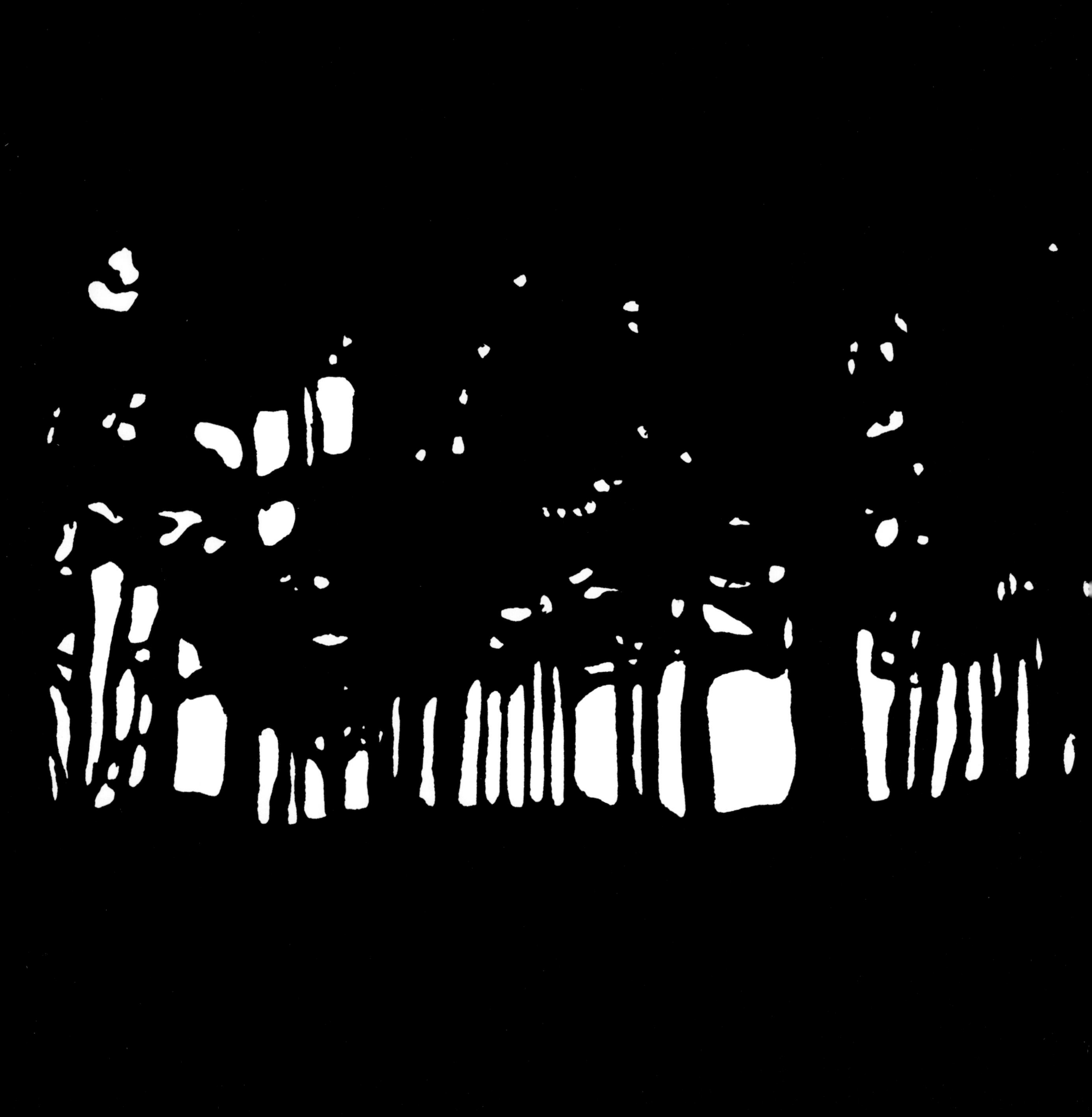

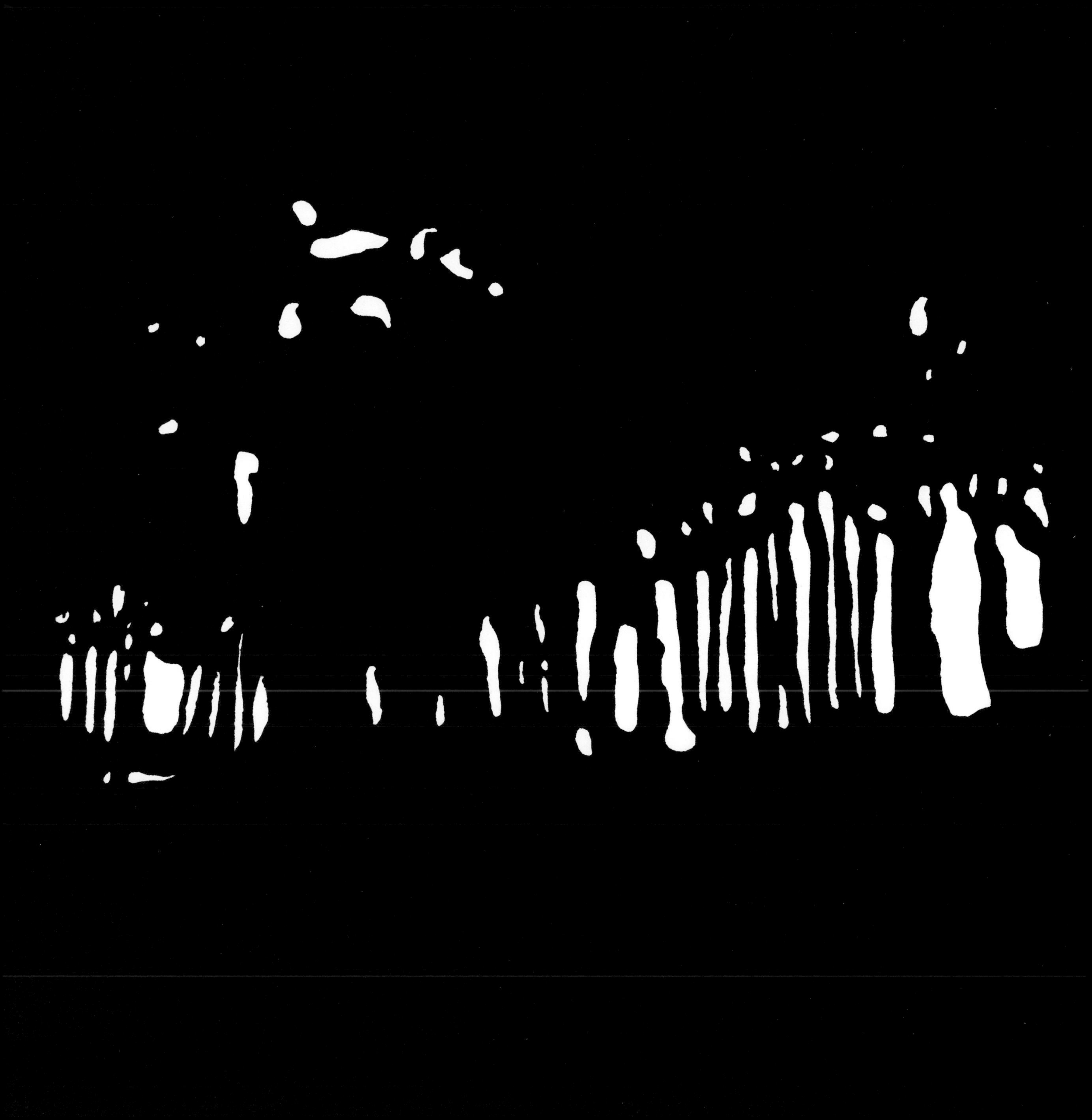

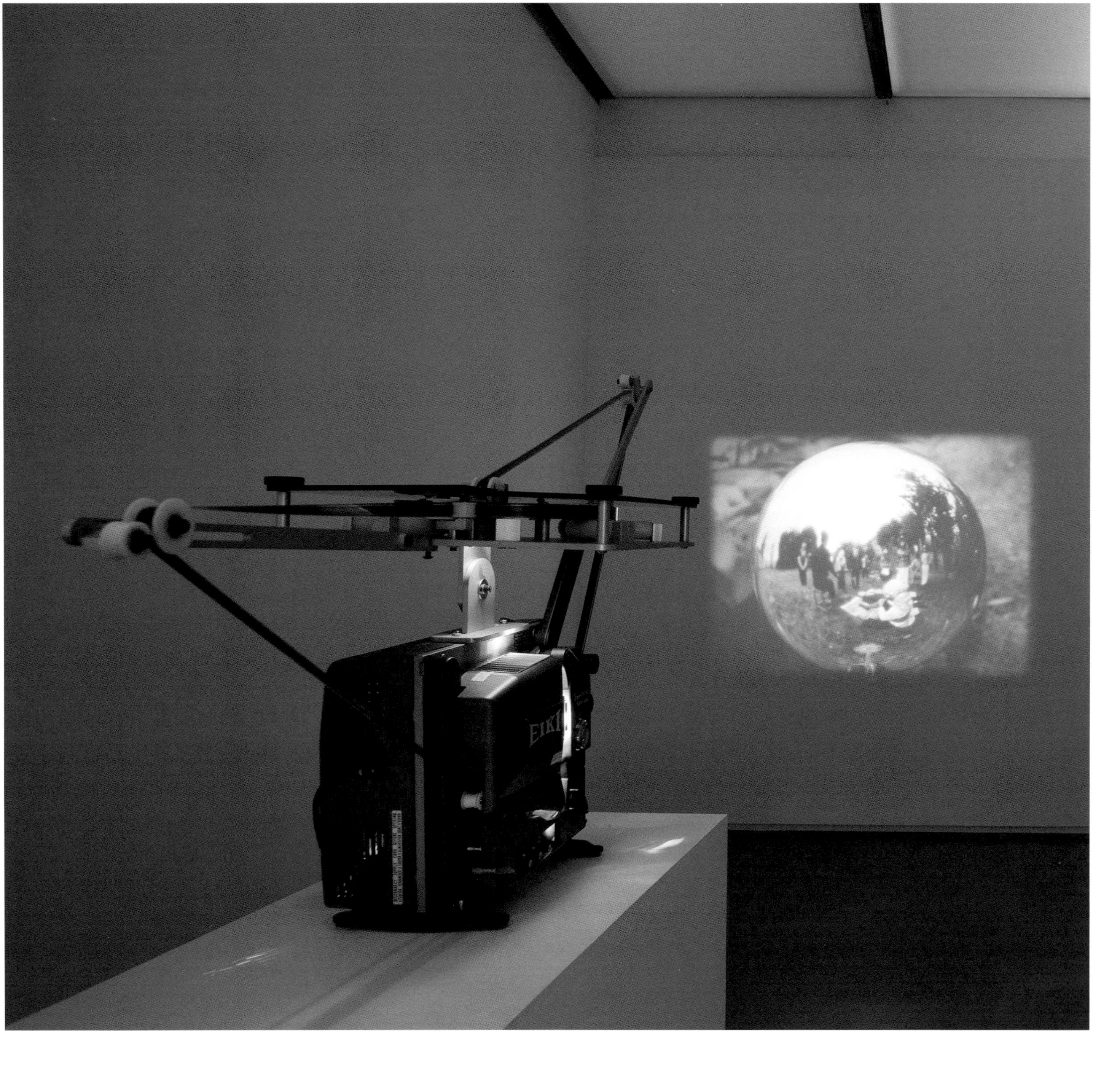
EIKI

Installation view: *Kugel (Ball)*, 2007
Still from *Geist (Ghost)*, 2007

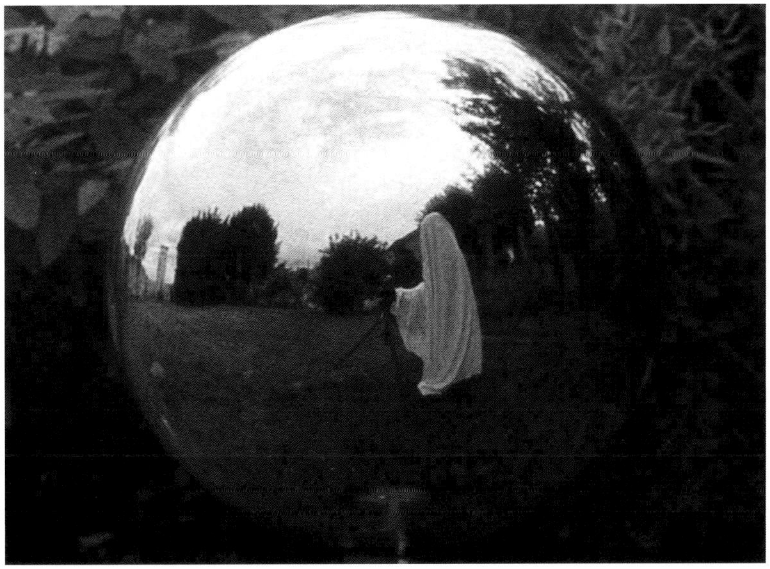

Still from *Geist (Ghost)*, 2007
Still from *Kugel (Ball)*, 2007
Overleaf *Quilt*, 2005

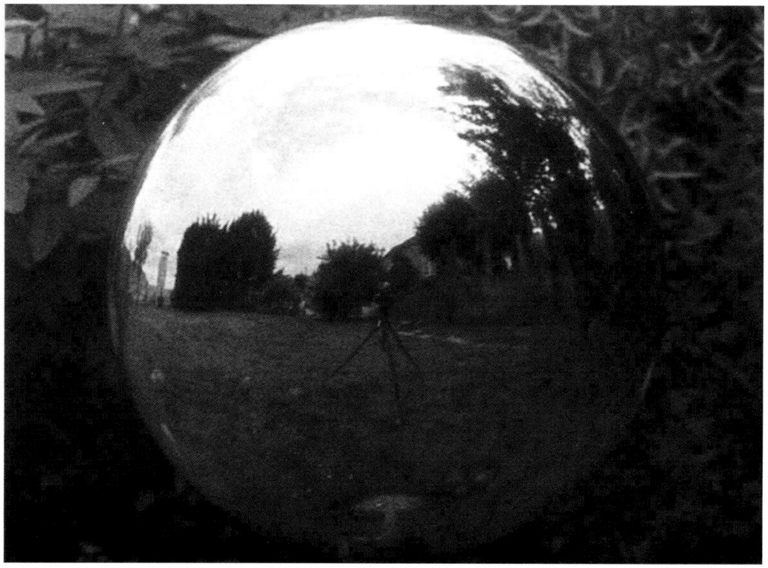

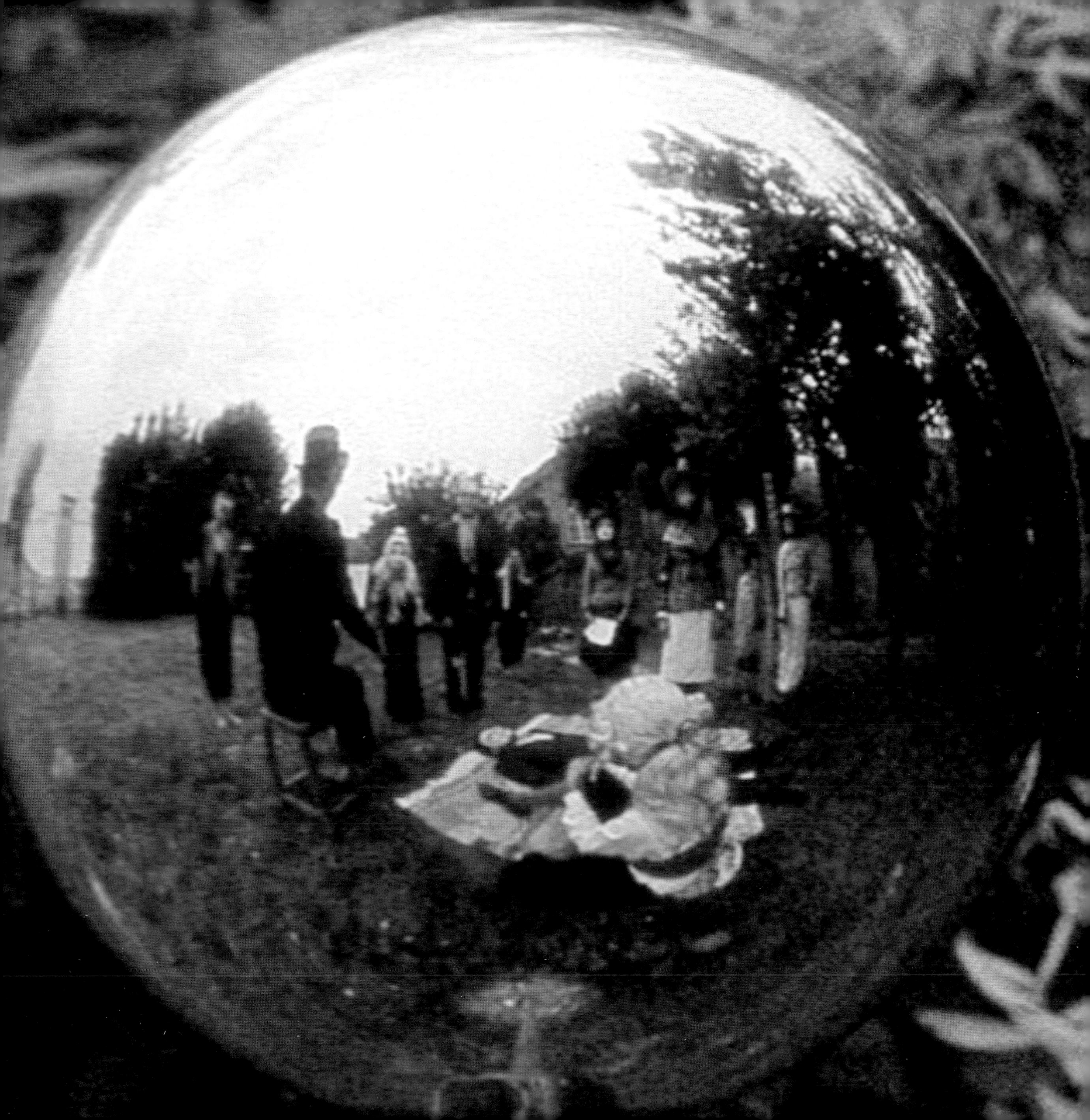

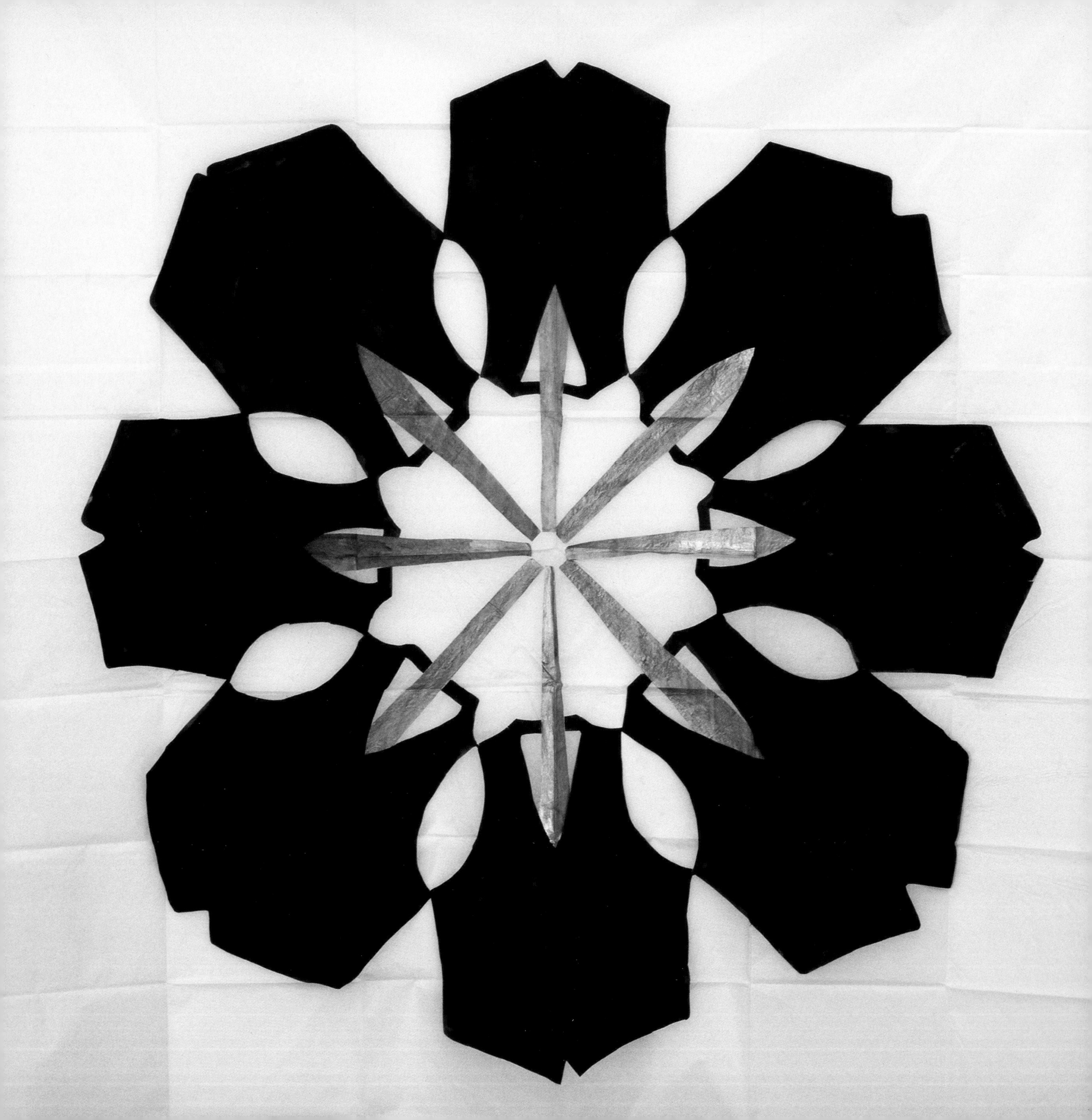

Mise en abyme

Beatrix Ruf

Ulla von Brandenburg operates with historical set pieces that vary widely in their origin and meaning. She finds them in literature, the visual arts, theatre, cinema and photography, as well as magazines, newspapers and flea markets. Her works, which, in addition to films, include drawings, silhouettes, watercolours, magazines, murals, objects, installations and performances, revolve around the identifiers of the 'rules' that govern constructions of social reality.

Von Brandenburg reverts back to material that accommodates the presence of the late 19th-century and the transition to so-called modernism, including its occultism, esotericism and psychoanalysis. In her discourse on collective contemporary experiences, she uses the 'cultivated' phenomena of this period, such as the theatre, the circus, magic, photography and film and, above all, pictorial compositions, e.g. collages, as formal filters that are not formed by a subjective artistic style.

However, von Brandenburg is not interested here in historical quotation per se or in the representation of a specific period or epoch, but in the enduring constants of codified behaviour, in the cultural transportation of social regularities and constellations and in the latent presences within these codes of identification, for example the unconscious – the irrational and the transgressive. In images of formalized action, she strips away both historical significance and ideologies and creates social choreographies that can generate new forms detached from their original content.

Central to her work are the repetition and permanence of the unchanging stories of the individual in the face of life, love and death in the history of the origins of civilization and apparent change, which represent the altering systems of belief and perceptual constructs within this history, and the cultural construction of our systems of perception.

The theatre features repeatedly in her work as a construct that reflects, demonstrates and permutates social forms, such as the codifications of the art form of theatre as the stage of life whose reality is pervaded by gestures, forms of behaviour and constructions of reality which define and position the individual in his or her perceptions, both in relation to him or herself and in relation to a social community. For example, through the use of a flat non-rectangular quasi-minimalist sculpture in the form of a chess-board in the work *Karo Sieben* (Seven of Diamonds, 2007) von Brandenburg demonstrates the central perspective of the theatre space. This not only conveys the tradition of Baroque theatre architecture, but also reflects socially hierarchical conditions; the theatre as a whole was always (and in most cases still is) structured around the seat of the king or ruler, whose place in the audience was definitive and permanent to the same extent that social hierarchies appeared to be inviolable.

The period of the late 19th-century and early 20th-century, from which much of von Brandenburg's motif world has been drawn, was also a time of great upheaval in the politics of perception. The new and increasing presence of the pictorial medium of photography introduced not only the notion of the representation of reality objectified by the machine, but also that of doubt about the visible world of things. A doubt that was due to both technical 'errors', such as the depiction of ghosts or ectoplasm in early photographs, but also the technical manipulability of the photographic image itself. As a result, there was a resurgence in the magical, the world of illusion and in the interest in the tricks and effects of the non-visible – both the objective aspects of reality and the psychological ones, for example in psychoanalysis. The medium of film, which was also new, intensified this aspect of photography in the dialogue between images, in the temporal sequence of images and also in the definition of the viewer and the audience's perception time. Von Brandenburg demonstrated this eloquently in her films *Ein Zaubertrickfilm* (2002) and *Around* (2005).

The field of tension between the theatre, the photographic moment and the temporal boundedness of film presented by von Brandenburg in her work accumulates in the constantly repeated *tableaux vivants* which she uses as both motivational and formal means in a series of films. Stillness and movement are paradoxically reversed here, as she turns the frozen image of the *tableaux vivants* into the temporal experience of the film. In these works, she plays with an entire series of opposite pairings: control and the loss of control (in relation to the actor's standing still for the image – a reference to the early history of photography when the film required lengthy exposure and hence motionless protagonists) or codified behaviour and the failure of control – the unpredictable, human, physical, emotional dimensions which refuse to submit to control. The *tableaux vivants* also demonstrate the field of tension between body language and absent language in a particularly impressive way – constituting, therefore, another reference to the beginnings of psycho-analysis. Sigmund Freud and Jean-Martin Charcot, with their research on hysteria, appear; the vocabulary of movements of the mind without language emerges. The figures in von Brandenburg's *tableaux vivants* are transfixed in the isolated gestures of a narrative. Filmic narrative methods, such as suspense, are used in a paradoxical way here. However, because of the tension between what is said and not said, the obvious symbolism and lack of narrative and meaningful connections to the expected next image are lacking; the story remains 'empty', released from linearity and development. And in a further nesting of gestures, codes, historical periods and reception models, she has the actors in her *tableaux vivants* appear in contemporary dress.

Von Brandenburg constantly 'releases' motifs from the theatre, film, photography, magic and the world of ghosts, the history of art and history of ideas, perceptual constructs and media effects, paralysed gestures of emotionality and interpersonal behaviour. She interweaves all of this in a large scale box-within-a-box to create a de-hierarchized collage, an endless mise en abyme, which makes it possible to experience the simultaneity of the durable and fragmentary nature of our experience in the theatre of being. And she also employs this nesting and immersion into a mise en abyme as a structuring element in her exhibitions: she usually combines murals, objects, installations, films and drawings to form a nested continuum of experiential spaces. You enter a world of images that, in turn, contain images and more images that, again and again, involve the same rules and symbols thatpermeate civilized life.

She often leads us into an exhibition, a central work in an exhibition or a work in a group exhibition through a curtain. This marks the entrance to a specialized experiential space which is familiar to us from other contexts, possibly that of the theatre, and also from symbolically complex contexts of social authority and intimacy or from the spiritual and religious context. Curtains indicate the distinguish ability of states of reality, for example the relation between the stage and life, the visible and concealed, symbolic control, the beginning and end of a temporally framed scene; they mark a break in the continuum of time. Curtains are dividing lines that visually mark the definitions of spaces and perceptual areas – they divide areas 'softly' on the level of visual and symbolic representation. Unlike the built wall, they make visible the transition from exterior to interior defined by architecture, from nature to culture; unlike the doors in built spaces – the endless nesting of reality-forming cultural codes and the continuum of power – we are in the same space of temporal, spatial and symbolical contexts. They are the perfect instrument for referring to the endless nesting of times, images, gestures, actions, meanings and contexts. *8* (2007), one of von Brandenburg's most recent installation works, whose title itself refers to the endlessness and indivisibility of beginning and end, represents an excellent example of this approach. Recorded in the Château de Chamarande close to Paris, the film shows an installation of hanging lengths of fabric, whose placement is based on the building's floor-plan, which are presented in eight different colours from the colour system developed by Swiss psychologist Max Lüscher, which has been in clinical use since 1947. The film leads us in a loop, which begins and ends a painting of the façade of the *château*, through its rooms, which – like the spatial sequence of an exhibition by von Brandenburg – contain images, objects and *tableaux vivants.*

All these are translations, representations and games with the symbolism of the endless loop and the title of the film itself. The handles of two walking sticks depicted lean closely against the wall to close the endless loop; fingers are intertwined in endless games with elastic bands; the hands of two protagonists cross, mirror images layer and continuously reproduce the rooms and figures, and so on. Installation, film, motif world, narrative on the mise en abyme of a complex layered image without beginning and end: 'whose beginning is not, nor end cannot be.'

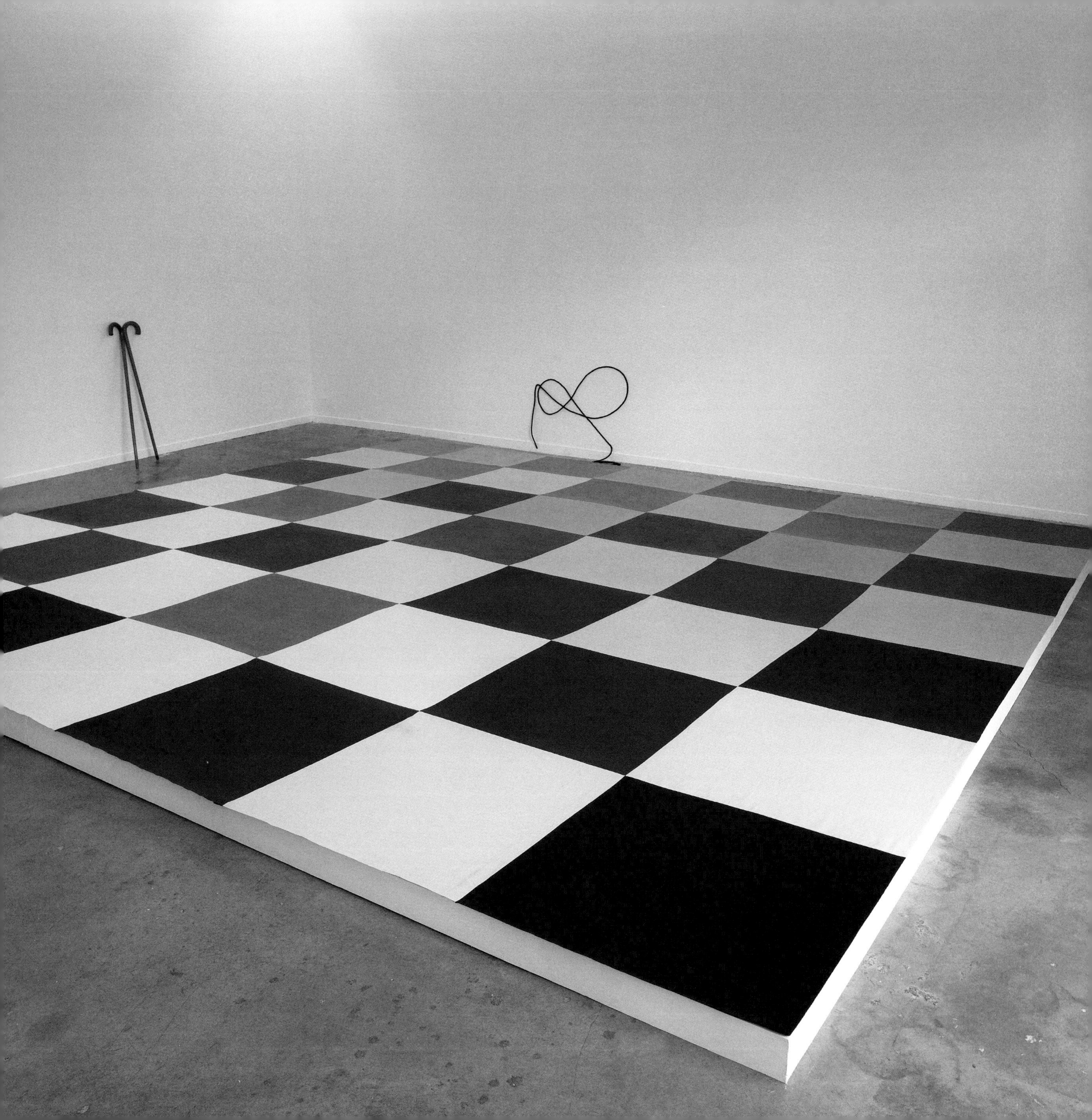

Installation views: *Karo Sieben (Seven of Diamonds)*, 2007

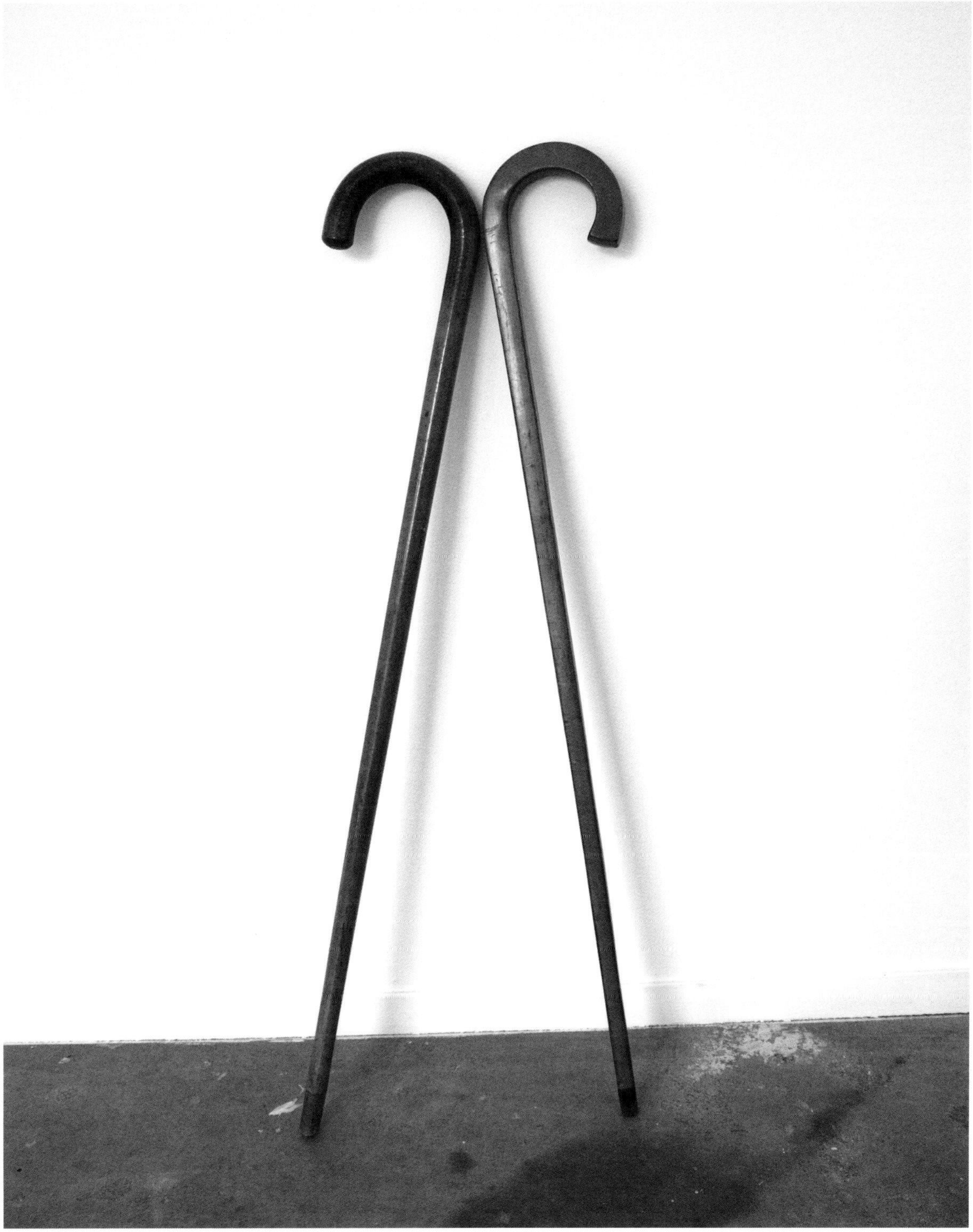

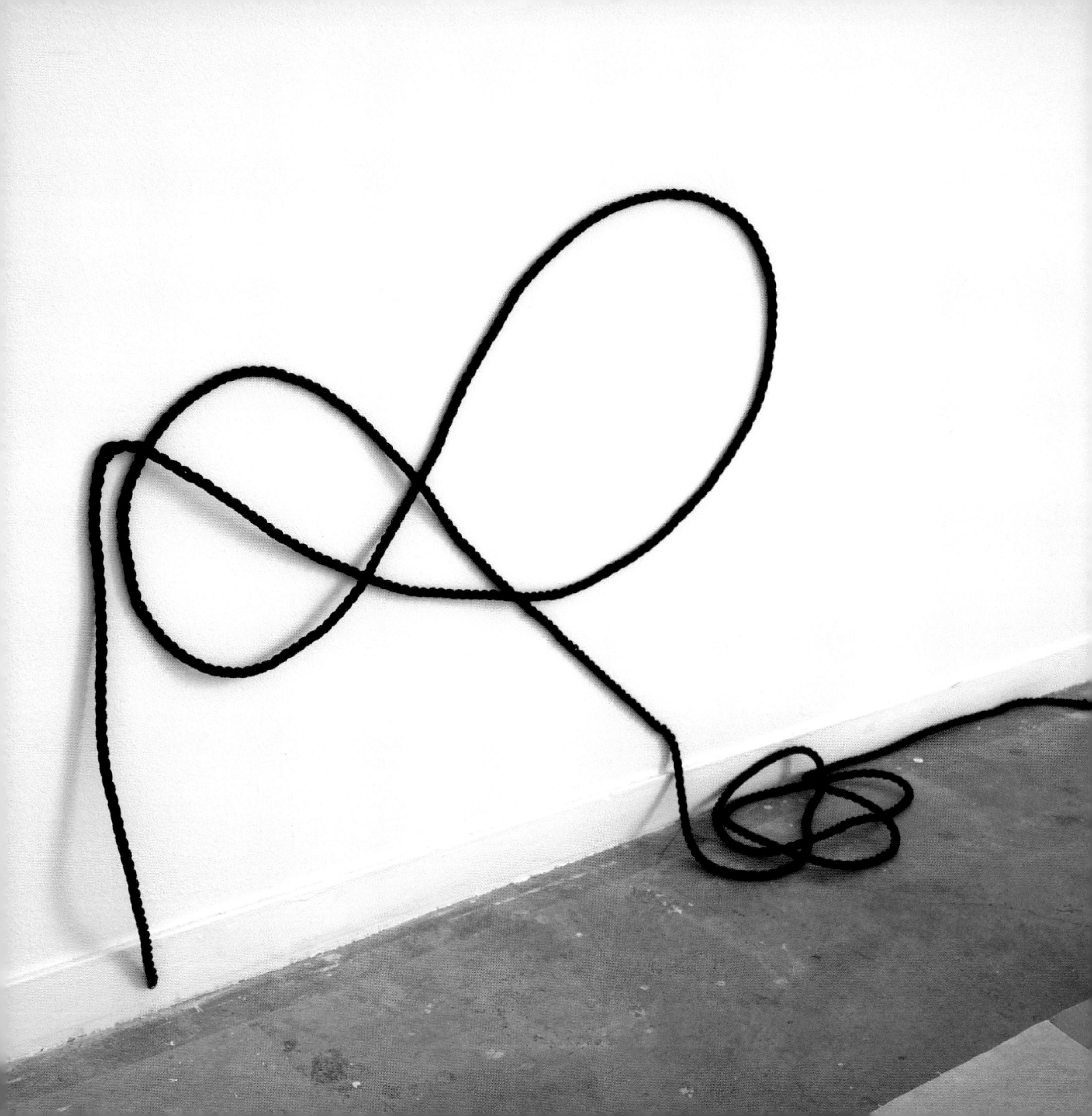

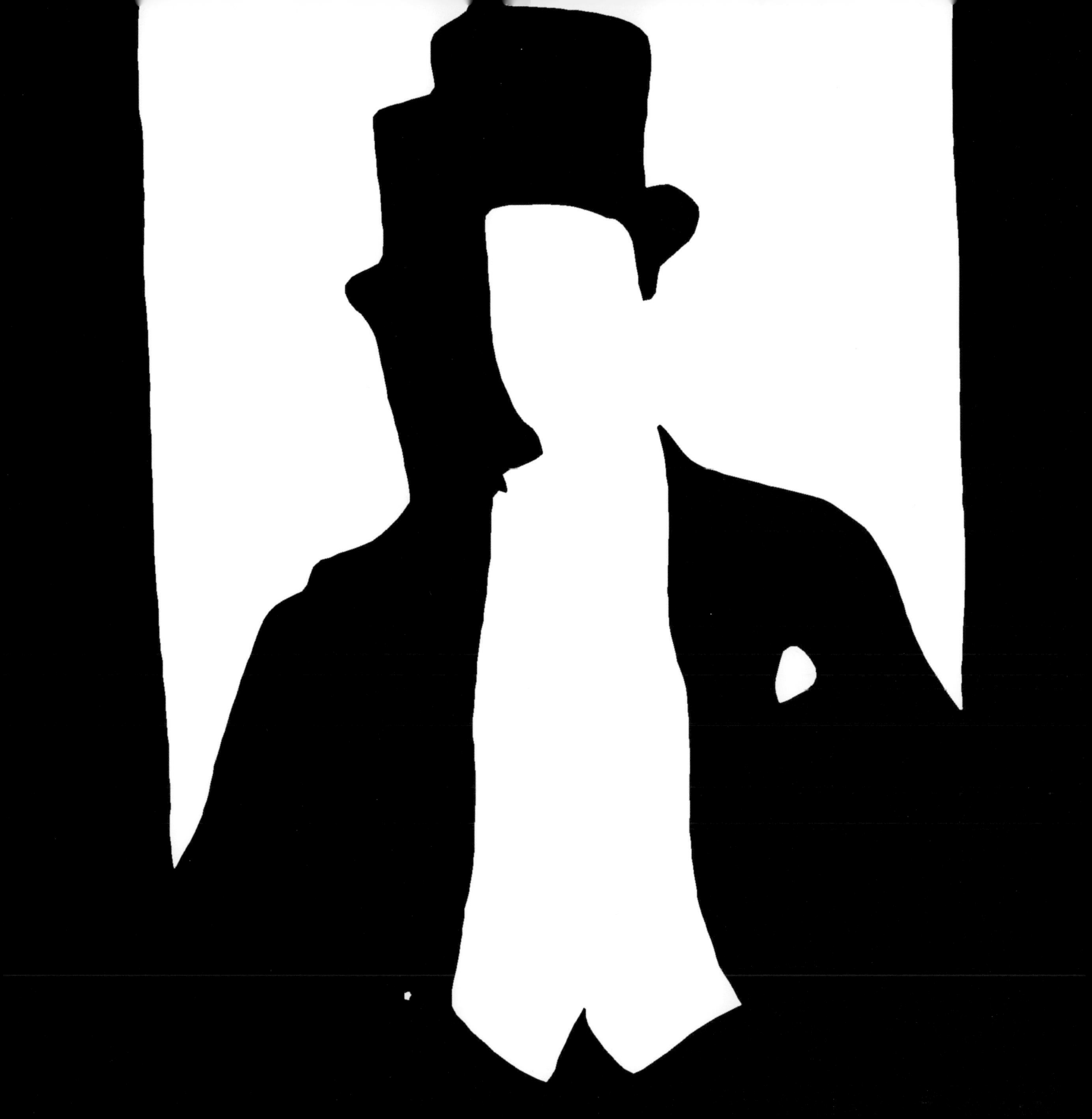

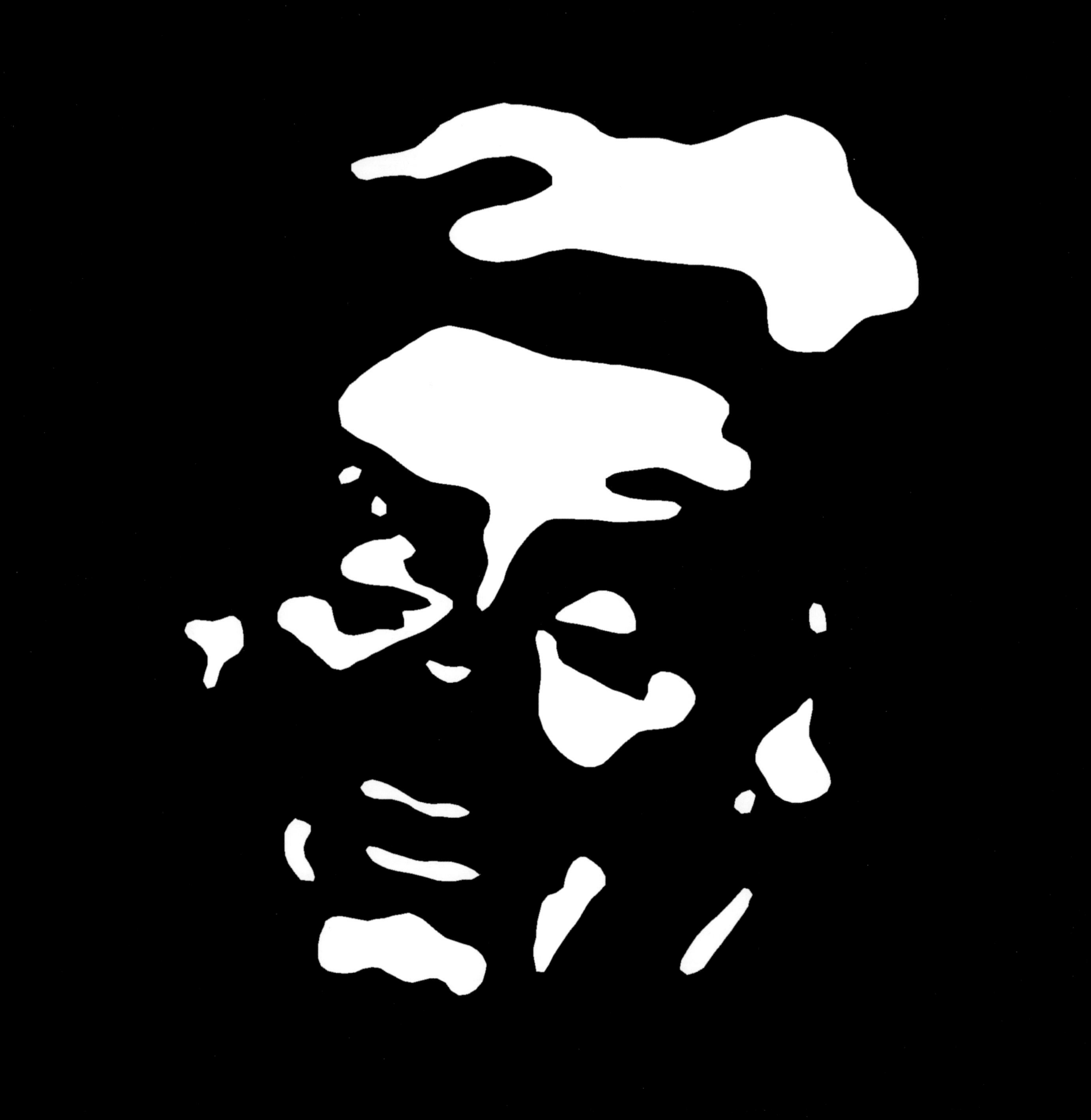

The Cherry Orchard

Excerpt from Chekhov's THE CHERRY ORCHARD
translated by Stephen Mulrine

Dramatis Personae

Lyubov RANEVSKAYA, *a landowner*
ANYA, *her daughter aged 17*
VARYA, *her adopted daughter, aged 24*
Leonid GAEV, *Ranevskaya's brother*
Yermolai LOPAKHIN, *a merchant*
Pyotr TROFIMOV, *a student*
Boris SIMEONOV-PISHCHIK, *a landowner*
CHARLOTTA Ivanovna, *a governess*
Semyon YEPIKHODOV, *a clerk*
DUNYASHA, *a maid*
FIRS, *an old servant, age 87*
YASHA, *a young servant*
A TRAMP, a STATIONMASTER, POST OFFICE CLERK,
various GUESTS *and* SERVANTS

The action takes place on Madame Ranevskaya's estate.

ACT THREE

The drawing-room, separated from the ballroom by an arch. It is evening, the chandelier is lit, and the Jewish band mentioned in Act Two can be heard playing in the hall. A 'grand-rond' is being danced in the ballroom, and PISHCHIK *calls out, 'Promenade à une paire!' The dancers come into the drawing-room, with* PISHCHIK *and* CHARLOTTA *leading, followed by* TROFIMOV *and* RANEVSKAYA, *then* ANYA *and a post-office* CLERK, VARYA *and the* STATIONMASTER, *etc.* VARYA *is quietly crying, wiping away her tears as she dances.* DUNYASHA *is in the last pair, and as they pass through the drawing-room,* PISHCHIK *shouts: 'Grand-rond, balancez!' and 'Les cavaliers à genoux et remerciez vos dames!'* FIRS, *wearing a tail-coat, brings in seltzer water on a tray.* PISHCHIK *and* TROFIMOV *then re-enter the drawing-room ...*

PISHCHIK
I've got rich blood, you see, I've already had two strokes- it makes dancing hard work, but you know what they say: if you run with the pack, you can bark if you like, but you've got to wag your tail. Anyway, I'm as strong as a horse. My late father, God rest him, was a great joker, and he used to say our ancestors, the original Simeonov-Pishchiks, were all descended from Caligula's horse, the one he made a senator. (*Sits*) Yes, trouble is, we've no money. And a hungry dog can't think of anything but meat ... (*Starts to snore, but instantly wakes up again.*) That's like me – all I can think about is money.

TROMFIMOV
Actually, you do look a bit like a horse.

PISHCHIK
Well, a horse is a fine animal. You can sell a horse.

In the adjoining room, a game of billiards is in progress. VARYA appears under the arch in the ballroom.

TROFIMOV (*teasing*)
Madame Lopakhin! Madame Lopakhin! ...

VARYA (*angrily*)
Huh, the mangy gent!

TROFIMOV
That's right – mangy, and proud of it!

VARYA (*bitterly*)
Oh yes, we can hire musicians, but how are we going to pay them? (*Exits*)

TROFIMOV (*to* PISHCHIK)
You know, you've spent your whole life looking for money to pay the interest on your debts, but if you'd put all that wasted energy to some other use, you could've turned the world upside-down by now.

PISHCHIK
Actually Nietzche – he's a famous philosopher, a great man, a huge intellect – he says somewhere that it's quite all right to forge banknotes.

TROMOFIMOV
You've read Nietzsche?

PISHCHIK
Well, no ... it was my Dasha that told me. The position I'm in now, I'd forge them in a minute. I've got to pay out three hundred and ten roubles, day after tomorrow. I've managed to get a hundred and thirty so far ... (*Feels in his pockets, alarmed.*) The money's gone! I've lost my money! (*In tears.*) Oh God, where is it! (*Then overjoyed.*) Here it is, it's inside the lining. Look I've broken out in a sweat ...

Enter RANEVSKAYA *and* CHARLOTTA.

RANEVSKAYA *is humming the 'Lezginka', a popular Caucasian folk-tune.*

RANEVSKAYA
I wonder what's keeping Leonid? What's he doing in town? Dunyasha, see if the musicians would like some tea.

TROFIMOV
The sale can't have gone ahead, most likely.

RANEVSKAYA
And the musicians came at the wrong time, we shouldn't have arranged this dance. Well, it doesn't matter ... (*Sits down and begins softly humming*).

CHARLOTTA (*offers* PISHCHIK *a pack of cards*).
Here you are, a pack of cards, think of a card, any one at all.

PISHCHIK
Right, I've thought of one.

CHARLOTTA
Now shuffle the pack. Good, that's fine. Now give it here, my dear Herr Pishchik. *Ein, zwei, drei!* There, now – look in your pocket ...

PISHCHIK (*takes the card out of his breast pocket*).
The eight of spades, that's absolutely right! Fancy that!

CHARLOTTA (*to* TROFIMOV, *holding the pack of cards on the palm of her hand*).
Quickly, what's the top card?

TROFIMOV
What? Oh, the Queen of spades.

CHARLOTTA
That's right! (*To* PISHCHIK.) Now then, what's the top card?

PISHCHIK
Ace of hearts.

CHARLOTTA
Right! (*She claps her hands and the pack of cards vanishes*) What lovely weather we're having!

She is answered by a mysterious female voice, apparently from under the floor: 'Oh yes, ma'am, it's magnificent.'

And you're so handsome, my ideal man ...

And the voice responds: 'And I am liking you too, ma'am.'

STATIONMASTER (*applauds*).
A lady ventriloquist, bravo!

PISHCHIK (*astonished*)
Well, fancy that! Charlotta Ivanovna, you're an absolute charmer – I'm quite in love ...

CHARLOTTA
In love? (*Shrugs.*) Can you love anybody? *Guter Mensch, aber schlechter Muzikant.*

TROFIMOV (*slaps* PISHCHIK on the back)
Yes, you're a horse all right.

CHARLOTTA
Please, pay attention – one more trick (*She picks up a travel-rug from a chair.*) Now, here's a rug, a fine travel rug for sale ... (*Shakes it out.*) Would anyone care to buy it?

PISHCHIK
Fancy that!

CHARLOTTA
Ein, zwei, dren!
She quickly lifts up the rug to reveal ANYA *standing behind it. She curtseys and runs to her mother, gives her a hug, then runs back into the ballroom to everyone's delight.*

RANEVSKAYA (*applauds*)
Bravo! Bravo!

CHARLOTTA
And now another one! *Ein zwei, drei ...*
She lifts up the rug to reveal VARYA, *who bows to the company.*

PISHCHIK
Fancy that!

CHARLOTTA
The end!

She flings the rug over PISHCHIK, *curtseys, and runs off to the ballroom.*

PISHCHIK (*following her out*)
What a rascal! What a woman, eh? (*Exits.*)

RANEVSKAYA
Still no sign of Leonid. What on earth's taking him so long? I mean, it's all been settled, the estate's either sold, or else the auction hasn't gone ahead, why's he keeping us in suspense all this time?

VARYA (*attempting to console her*)
Our uncle will have bought it, I'm sure of that.

TROFIMOV (*mockingly*)
Oh, for sure.

VARYA
The Countess has given him power of attorney, to buy it in her name and take over the mortgage. She's done it for Anya's sake. God will help us, I'm sure of it – uncle'll buy it.

RANEVSKAYA
Your great-aunt in Yaroslavl sent fifteen thousand roubles, to buy the property in her name – that's how much she trusts us – and that's not even enough to pay off the interest (*Covers her face with her hands.*) Well, my fate's being decided today, yes, indeed.

TROFIMOV (*teasing* VARYA)
Madame Lopakhin!

VARYA (*angrily*)
Eternal student! That's twice already you've been kicked out of university.

RANEVSKAYA
Varya, why are you so angry? He's only teasing about Lopakhin, what's wrong with that? Marry Lopakhin, if you like – he's very nice, an interesting man. And if you don't like, then don't marry him. Nobody's forcing you, my pet.

VARYA
Mama, I take this very seriously, and I'll say it straight out – yes, he's a good man, and I do like him.

RANEVSKAYA
Then marry him. I don't know what you're waiting for.

VARYA
Mama, I can't propose to him myself, can I. People have been talking about him for two years now, everybody has, but he either says nothing, or else he makes a joke about it. And I can see why. He's too busy getting rich, he's no time for me. And If I had any money, even just a little, a hundred roubles even, I'd give it all up and clear off. I'd go into a convent.

TROFIMOV
A life of bliss!

VARYA (*to* TROFIMOV)
You'd think a student'd have more sense! (*Then gently in tears.*) You've grown so ugly, Petya – so old. (*To* RANEVSKAYA, *no longer crying.*) But I can't stand to be idle, Mama. I need to be doing something, every minute of the day.

Enter YASHA

YASHA (*trying not to laugh*)
Yepikhodov's just broken a billiard cue! (*Exits.*)

VARYA
What's Yepikhodov doing here? Who gave him permission to play billiards? Honestly, I don't understand these people ... (*Exits.*)

RANEVSKAYA
Petya, you shouldn't tease here – you can see she's got enough trouble.

TROFIMOV
Well, she makes such a fuss, she's always interfering in other people's business. She hasn't given us a minute's peace the whole summer, Anya and me. She's scared we might fall in love or something. And what's it got to do with her? It's not as if I've given her any grounds, I'm past all that vulgar rubbish. We're beyond love.

RANEVSKAYA
Then I suppose I must be beneath love. (*Extremely agitated.*) Why isn't Leonid here? If only I knew whether the estate's been sold or not! It's a disaster, it seems so incredible that I don't know what to think, I'm completely at a loss. I could start screaming right now, do something really stupid. Petya, you've got to save me. Talk to me, say something ...

TROFIMOV
Whether it's been sold or not today, does it really matter? It's finished and done with, there's no way back – that path's long since overgown. You might as well give up, dear lady. There's no point in deceiving yourself, you need to face the truth, even just once in your life.

RANEVSKAYA
What truth? Maybe you can see what's truth, and what isn't, but I've lost my sight, I can't see anything. Yes, you can solve all the great problems, but that's because you're too young to have suffered, to have experienced any problems of your own – isn't that so, darling?

You can look boldly ahead, because you can't see anything to be frightened of, you're not expecting it, no, because life, real life, is still hidden from your young eyes. So you're braver, more honest, more profound than us, but just stop to think, if you have a generous bone in your whole body, show me some compassion. I was born here, you know, my mother and father, my grandfather lived here, and I love this house, I can't conceive of my life without the cherry orchard, and if it has to be sold now, well, you might as well sell me along with it ... (*Embraces* TROFIMOV, *kisses him on the forehead.*) Good God, my son was drowned here ... (*Weeps.*) Have pity on me, my dear, kind friend.

TROFIMOV
You know I feel for you with all my heart.

RANEVSKAYA
But you must say it, tell me some other way ... (*She takes out her handkerchief, and a telegram falls onto the floor.*) I've got so much on my mind today, you can't imagine. It's so noisy in here, my heart jumps at every sound, I'm trembling all over, but I can't go to my own room, I'm afraid of the silence when I'm alone. Petya, don't be too hard on me ... I love you like a son, and I'd willingly let you marry Anya, believe me I would, but, darling, you have to study, you have to finish your degree. You're not doing anything, you're just tossed by fate from one place to the next, it's very strange. Well, it's the truth, isn't it? And you really ought to do something about that beard, to make it grow a bit ... (*Laughs.*) You look so funny!

TROFIMOV (*picking up the telegram*)
I've no desire to be handsome.

RANEVSKAYA
That's a telegram from Paris. I get one every day. Yesterday and today. That crazy man's fallen sick again, he's in real trouble ... He wants to forgive him, begs me to return, and I really ought to go back to Paris, to be by his side. You look very grim, Petya, but what can I do, my darling, honestly, what can I do – he's ill, he's all alone and miserable, and who's going to look after him, who'll keep him out of the harm's way, who'll give him his medicine on time? I love him, and that's that ... He's a millstone round my neck, and he's dragging me down with him but I love him just the same, I can't live without him. (*Squeezes* TROFIMOV's *hand.*) Don't think badly of me, Petya, don't say a word, please don't ...

TROFIMOV (*emotionally*)
God forgive me for speaking out, but I've got to – the man's robbing you blind!

RANEVSKAYA
No, no, don't say things like that!

TROFIMOV
He's a scoundrel, and you're the only one who can't see it! He's a worthless nonentity ...

RANEVSKAYA (*angry, but in control of herself*)
And you're twenty-six or twenty-seven, and still a schoolboy.

TROFIMOV
So what if I am?

RANEVSKAYA
It's time you grew up – at your age you ought to have some understanding of people in love.

You need to love someone yourself – yes, you need to fall in love, Petya! (*Angrily.*) That's right! And that purity of yours is nothing but a pose – you're a ridiculous crank, a freak ...

TROFIMOV (*aghast*)
How can you say that!

RANEVSKAYA
I'm beyond love!' No, you're not beyond love, you're just plain daft, as old Firs would say. At your age, not even to have a mistress!

TROFIMOV
This is dreadful! How can you say that! (*He hurries out to the ballroom, clutching his head.*) It's just dreadful ... I can't stand it, I've got to go ... (*Exits, then immediately re-enters.*) We're finished, do you hear! (*Exits to the hall.*)

RANEVSKAYA (*shouts after him*)
Petya, wait!
Don't' be silly, I was only joking! Petya!
Outside in the hall, the sound of someone running upstairs, and suddenly falling back down with a great crash. ANYA *and* VARYA *shriek, then immediately burst out laughing.*

What's going on!

ANYA *rushes in laughing.*

ANYA
It's Petya – he's fallen downstairs! (*Runs out again.*)

RANEVSKAYA
What a strange boy he is.

Meanwhile the STATIONMASTER *stands in the middle of the ballroom, and begins reciting Aleksei Tolstoy's poem 'The Sinner'. Everyone stops to listen, but he has hardly spoken a few lines when a waltz is stuck up in the hall, and the recital is interrupted, as the dancing begins.* TROFIMOV, ANYA, VARYA *and* RANEVSKAYA *come in from the hall.*

Come on, Petya ... pure of heart ... please forgive me. Come, let's dance ...

She begins dancing with TROFIMOV, *and* ANYA *dances with* VARYA. FIRS *enters, and leans his walking-stick against the side door.* YASHA *also enters from the drawing-room, to watch the dancing.*

YASHA
Well, how are things, old man?

FIRS
Not great. Time was, we had generals, and barons and admirals at our dances, now we've got to send for the post-office clerk and the stationmaster, yes, and they're not that keen to come, neither. I'm feeling a bit weak, myself. The old master, her granddad, he used to make us take sealing-wax, for any sort of illness. I've taken sealing-wax every day for the last twenty years or more. Maybe it's that what's kept me alive.

YASHA
You give me a pain, old man. (*Yawns.*) It's about time you snuffed it.

FIRS
Huh! And you're just daft! (*Mutters.*)

TROFIMOV *and* RANEVSKAYA *are dancing in the ballroom, then move into the drawing-room.*

RANEVSKAYA
Merci. I'll sit down for bit ... (*Sits down.*) I'm tired.

Enter ANYA, *very agitated.*

ANYA. There was somebody in the kitchen just now – he says the cherry orchard's been sold.

RANEVSKAYA
Sold to whom?

ANYA
He didn't say. And now he's gone.

She begins dancing with TROFIMOV, and they exit to the ballroom.

YASHA
It was some old man raving on. Nobody we know.

FIRS
And the master's not home yet. He's wearing his light overcoat, too – he'll catch cold, like as not. Huh, these young people they've no sense.

RANEVSKAYA
Honestly, I could die right now. Yasha, go and find out who it was sold to.

YASHA
He's cleared off long ago, the old goat. (*Laughs.*)
RANEVSKAYA (*slightly irritated*). What are you laughing at? What are you so happy about?

YASHA
It's that Yepikhodov – he really is a scream. He's so stupid – the walking disaster.

RANEVSKAYA
So, where will you go, Firs, If the estate's sold?

FIRS
I'll go wherever you tell me, ma'am.

RANEVSKAYA
Why are you looking like that? Are you unwell? You know, you really ought to be in bed …

FIRS
Oh, yes … (*With a hint of mockery.*) and if I go to bed, who's going to hand things round, and look after everybody? There's only me, in the whole house.

YASHA (*to* RANEVSKAYA)
Madame, permit me to make a request of you, if you'd be so kind! If you're going back to Paris, please do me a favour and take me with you. I can't stay here, it's absolutely impossible. (*Looking round, in an aside.*)
I mean, I don't need to tell you, you can see for yourself, this is a backward country, the people have no morals, and it's so boring! The food in the kitchen's disgusting, and that Firs creature goes round muttering the whole time, he doesn't make any sense. Take me with you, ma'am, please!

Enter PISHCHIK.

PISHCHIK
May I have the honour, fair lady, of this little waltz? (RANEVSKAYA *goes off with him.*) You're quite enchanting, but if I could borrow a hundred and eighty roubles from you … well, if I could … A hundred and eighty, that's all …

They begin dancing and pass through into the ballroom.

YASHA (*sings softly*)
'Oh, can't you see how troubled is my heart …'

A figure appears in the ballroom, wearing a grey top-hat, and checked trousers. Shouts of 'Bravo, Charlotta Ivanovna!, as she flings her arms about and jumps in the air.

DUNYASHA (*stops to powder her nose*)
Well, Firs Nikolaevich, the mistress ordered me to dance – there's too many gentlemen and not enough ladies – but dancing makes me dizzy, and my heart's pounding.

And that post-office clerk's just said something that's taken my breath away.
The music dies down.

FIRS
So what did he say?

DUNYASHA
You're like a little flower, he said.

YASHA (*yawns*)
Ignorant peasant ... (*Exits.*)

DUNYASHA
Like a flower ... You know, I'm quite a sensitive person, I'm terribly fond of compliments.

FIRS
You'll get your head turned, you will.

Enter YEPIKHODOV.

YEPIKHODOV
It's obvious you don't want to see me, Dunyasha – it's as if I was some sort of insect (*Sighs.*) Oh, what a life!

DUNYASHA
What do you want?

YEPIKHODOV
Well, no doubt you're right. (*Sighs.*) On the other hand, of course, looking at it from a point of view, then you – if I may permit myself to say so, and excuse my frankness – you've completely reduced me to a state of mind. I know my own destiny – every day some new disaster befalls me, I've got well used to it, so I can look upon my fate with a smile. But you gave me your word, and although I...

DUNYASHA
Please, let's talk later – just leave me in peace. I'm in a dream now. (*Toying with her fan.*)

YEPIKHODOV
Yes some new mishap every day, and if you'll allow me to say so, I just smile – laugh, even.

VARYA *enters from the ballroom.*

VARYA
Are you still here, Yepikhodov? You really are an ill-mannered wretch. (*To* DUNYASHA.) You'd better go, Dunyasha. (*To* YEPIKHODOV.) First you break a cue playing billiards, now you're strolling round the drawing-room like an invited guest!

YEPIKHODOV
If you'll allow me to say so, I don't think you can sue me for damages.

VARYA
I'm not suing you, I'm telling you! You do nothing but wander from one place to the next, you never do any work. We employ a clerk, but God only know what for.

YEPIKHODOV (*offended*)
Whether I work or walk about, yes, or eat, or play billiards, that's a matter for older and wiser heads to judge – more understanding ...

VARYA (*explodes*)
You dare say that to me! You dare! You think I don't understand? Get out of here! Go one, get out!

YEPIKHODOV (*cringing*)
Please express yourself a little more delicately ...

VARYA (*beside herself*)
If you don't get out of my sight this instant ... Out! Out!

VARYA *pursues him to the door.*

Walking disaster! Now get out and stay out! Don't let me see you in this house every again!

YEPIKHODOV *exits, shouts from behind the door: 'I'm going to complain about you!'*

Oho, coming back in, are you? (*Seizes FIRS' walking-stick from beside the door.*) Come on ... Come on, then, and I'll show you ... Are you coming in? Eh? Take that! (*Swings the stick just as* LOPAKHIN *comes through the door.*)

LOPAKHIN
Why, thank you, most humbly!

VARYA (*annoyed, sarcastically*)
I beg your pardon.

LOPAKHIN
Don't mention it. I'm most grateful for such a warm reception.

VARYA
It's not worth your gratitude. (*Walks away, then looks round and asks gently.*) I didn't hurt you, did I?

LOPAKHIN
No, not at all. I'll have an enormous bump, that's all. *Voices are heard in the ballroom: 'Lopakhin's arrived! He's here now!*

PISHCHIK
The very same, large as life! (*Embraces* LOPAKHIN.) There's a faint whiff of brandy about you, my dear chap. And we've been enjoying ourselves here too.

Enter RANEVSKAYA.

RANEVSKAYA
Lopakhin, is that you? What kept you so long? Where's Leonid?

LOPAKHIN
He came home with me, he's just ...

RANEVSKAYA (*agitated*)
Well, what happened? Was it sold? Tell me!

LOPAKHIN (*embarrassed, trying not to show his delight*)
The auction was over by four o'clock ... We missed the train, so we had to wait till half-past nine ... (*A deep sigh.*) Phew, I feel a bit dizzy ...

Enter GAEV. *He is carrying some parcels in one hand, and wiping away tears with the other.*

RANEVSKAYA
What's the matter, Leo? Leo, what is it? (*Impatiently, in tears.*) For God's sake, tell me!

GAEV *doesn't answer, waves his hand despairingly.*

GAEV (*to* FIRS, *weeping*)
Here, take these ... There's some anchovies, and fresh herrings ... I've had nothing to eat all day ... Oh, God, what I've gone through ...

The billiard room door is open, and we can hear the click of billiard balls, and the voice of YASHA: *'That's seven, and eighteen!'* GAEV'S *expression has changed, and he is no longer weeping.*

I'm dreadfully tired. Help me get changed, Firs. (Exits to his own room through the ballroom, followed by FIRS.)

PISHCHIK
So, what about the auction? Come on, tell us!

RANEVSKAYA
Has the cherry orchard been sold?

LOPAKHIN
Yes.

RANEVSKAYA
Who bought it?

LOPAKHIN
I did.

A silence. RANEVSKAYA *is overwhelmed. If it weren't for the table and chair beside here, she would fall down.* VARYA *detaches the keys from her belt, flings them to the floor in the middle of the drawing-room, and walks out.*

I bought it! Ladies and gentlemen, please, wait – I've a bit of a thick head, I can't speak ... (*Laughs.*) When we got to the auction, Deriganov was already there. Leonid Andreyich had only fifteen thousand, and straight away Deriganov bid another thirty, on top of the mortgage. Well, I could see how things were going, so I waded in with forty thousand. He went up to forty-five, so I bid fifty-five. He would go up by five, you see, and I'd bid another ten. Well, it finished eventually. I bid ninety thousand roubles over and above the mortgage, and it was knocked down to me. The cherry orchard's mine now. All mine! (*Laughs.*) Tell me I'm drunk, or crazy, tell me I'm imagining all this ... (*Stamps his feet.*) No, don't laugh at me! If only my father and grandfather could rise up out of their graves, and see all that's happened – how their little Yermolai, their abused, semi-literate Yermolai, who used to run around barefoot in winter – how that same Yermolai has bought this estate, the most beautiful spot on earth. Yes, I've bought the land on which my father and grandfather were slaves, where they weren't even allowed into the kitchen. I must be asleep, it's all just a dream, it's all in the mind ... It's your imagination at work, shrouded in mystery ... (*Picks up the keys, smiling affectionately.*) She threw down the keys, to show she's no longer mistress of this house. (*Jingles the keys.*) Well, it doesn't matter.

The musicians are heard tuning up.

Hey, musicians, let's hear you play! Come on in, all of you, and watch Yermolai Lopakhin take his axe to the cherry orchard, see the trees falling down! We're going to build cottages here, and our grandsons and great-grandsons'll see a whole new life ... Come on, let's have some music!

The orchestra starts playing. RANEVSKAYA *slumps into a chair, weeping bitterly.* LOPAKHIN *reproaches her.*

Why didn't you listen to me, eh? Why not? Oh, my poor dear lady, there's no going back now. (*A catch in his voice.*) God, I wish all this was over and done with, I wish our miserable, disjointed lives could be somehow changed.

PISHCHIK (*takes him by the arm, whispers*)
She's crying. Let's go into the ballroom, and leave her be ... Come on ... (*Leads* LOPAKHIN *towards the ballroom.*)

LOPAKHIN
What's going on? Hey, musicians, play up so we can hear you! Everything's to be as I want it. (*Ironically.*) Come on, here comes the new landlord, the owner of the cherry orchard! (*Accidentally bumps into a table, almost knocks over the candelabra.*) What the hell, I can pay for it! (*Exits with* PISHCHIK.)

There is no-one left now in the ballroom or drawing-room, apart from RANEVSKAYA, *who sits hunched up, still weeping bitterly. The orchestra plays quietly in the background.* ANYA *and* TROFIMOV *come running in.* ANYA *goes up to her mother and kneels down before her.* TROFIMOV remains by the ballroom door.

ANYA
Mama! Mama, you're crying! Oh, my dear, kind, good Mama, darling Mama, I love you so much … God bless you, Mama. The cherry orchard's sold, it's all gone now, it's true, it's true, but don't cry, Mama, please – you still have your life in front of you, you still have your good, pure heart … Come with me, darling mama, we'll leave here, we'll go away together. We can plant a new orchard somewhere, even more beautiful, and when you see it, you'll understand, and joy – a deep, quiet joy will descend on your soul, Mama, like the sun in the evening, and you'll smile again … Come, my darling … Come …

Curtain

Tarot: 7 d' épeé (7 of Swords), 2008

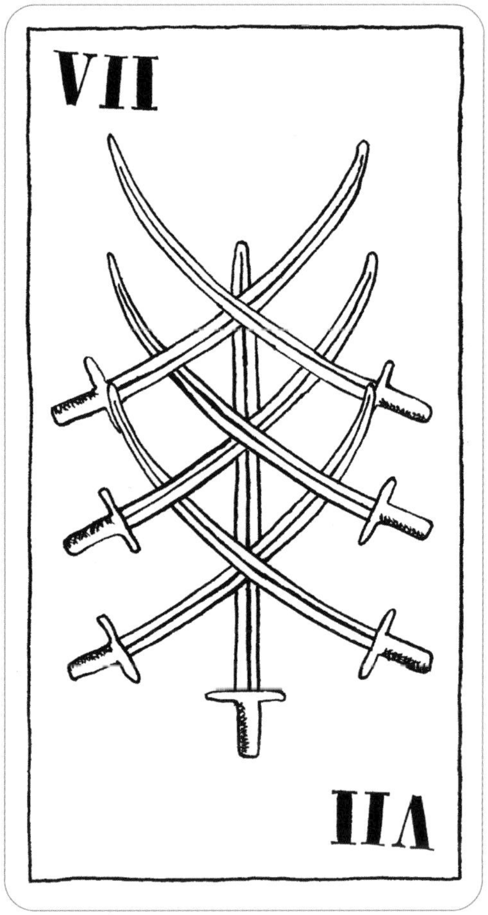

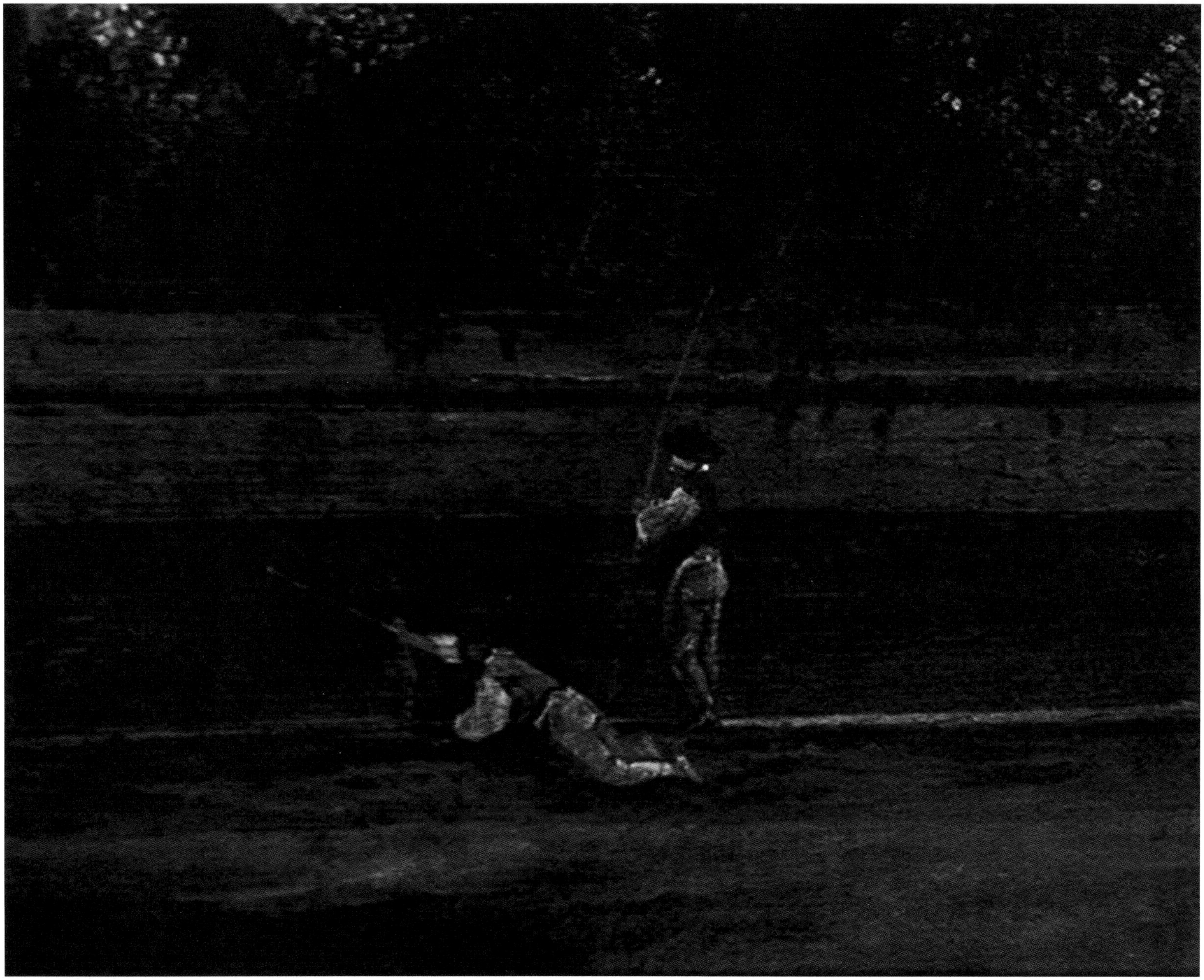

Stills from *8*, 2007

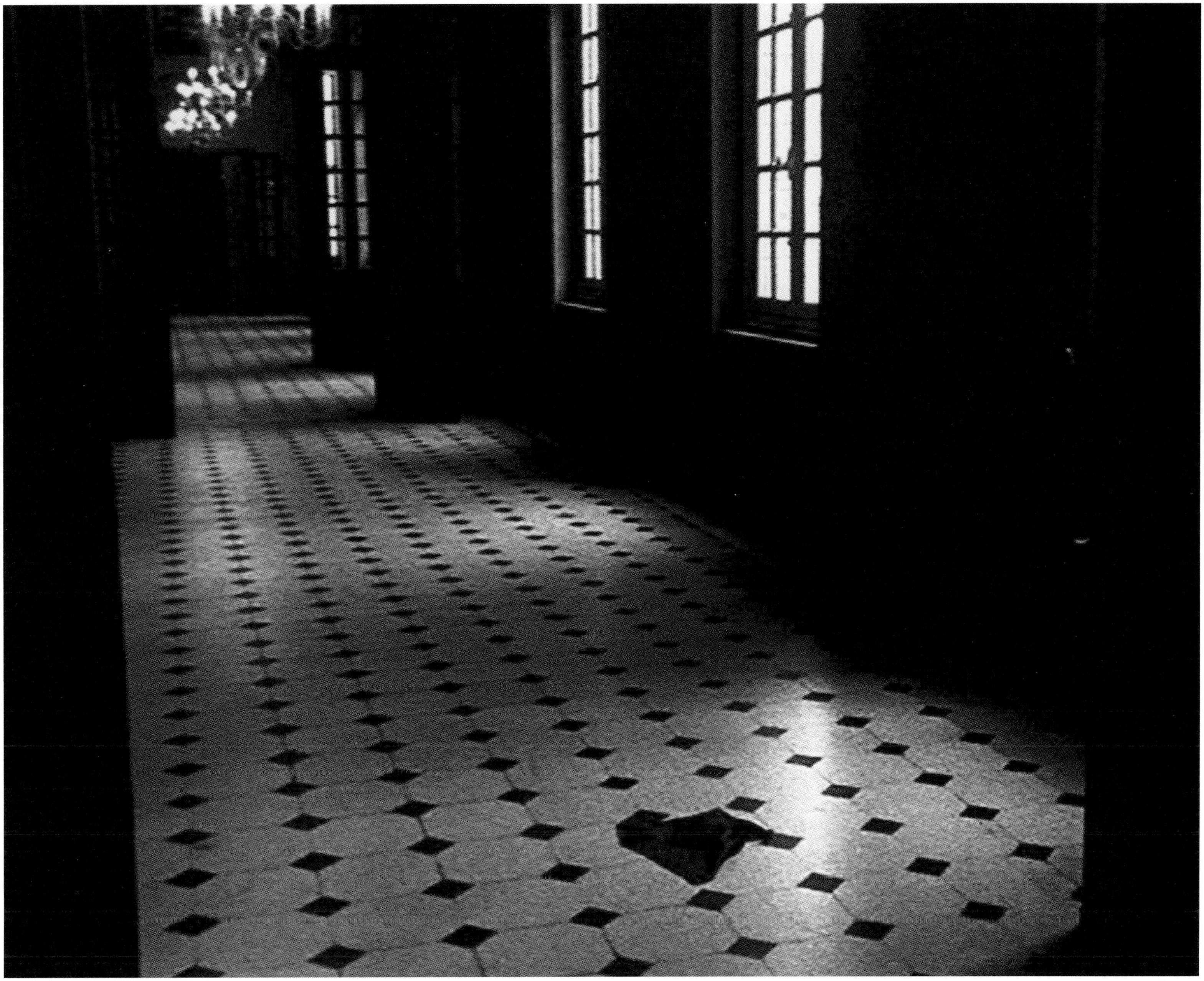

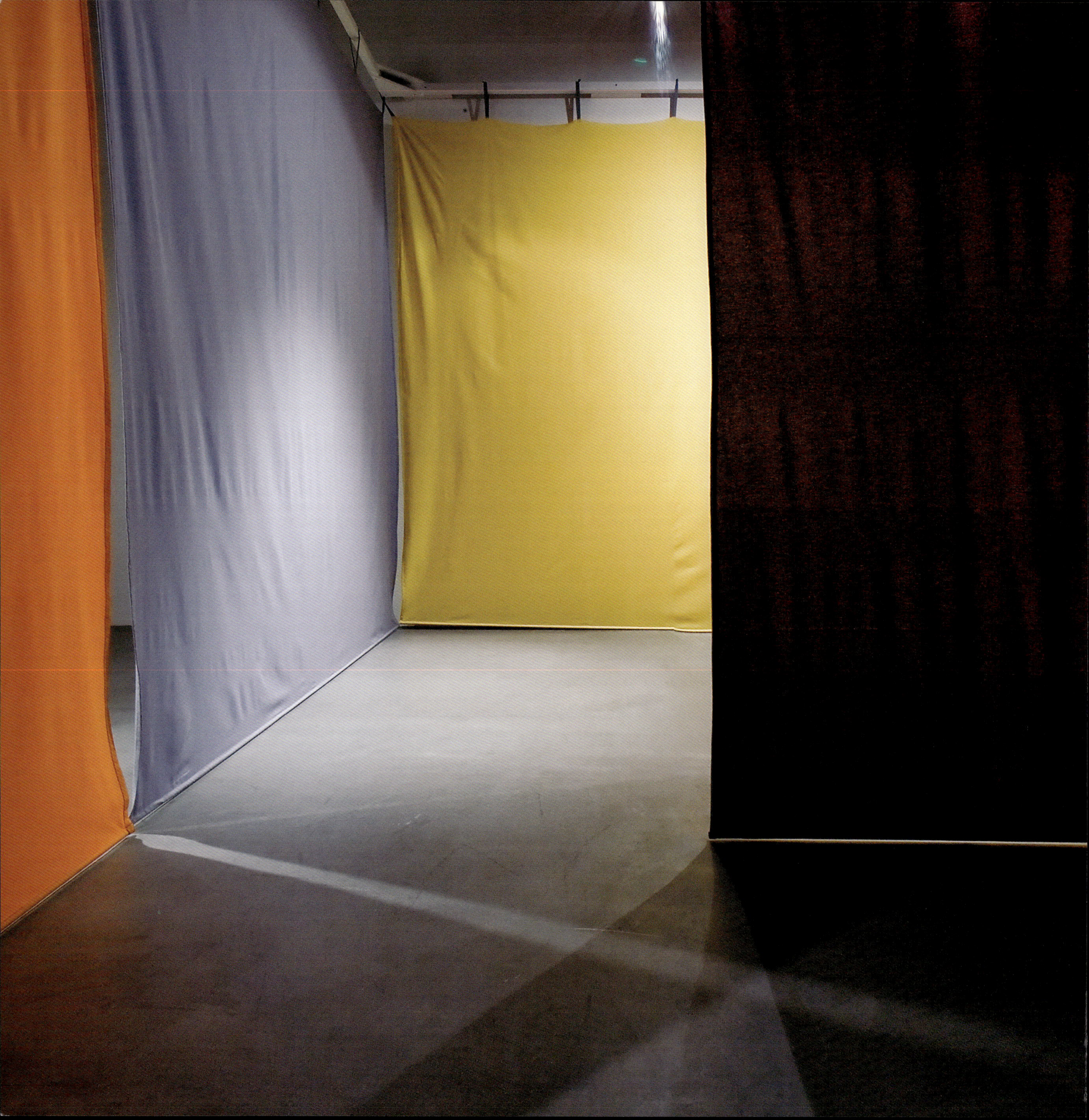

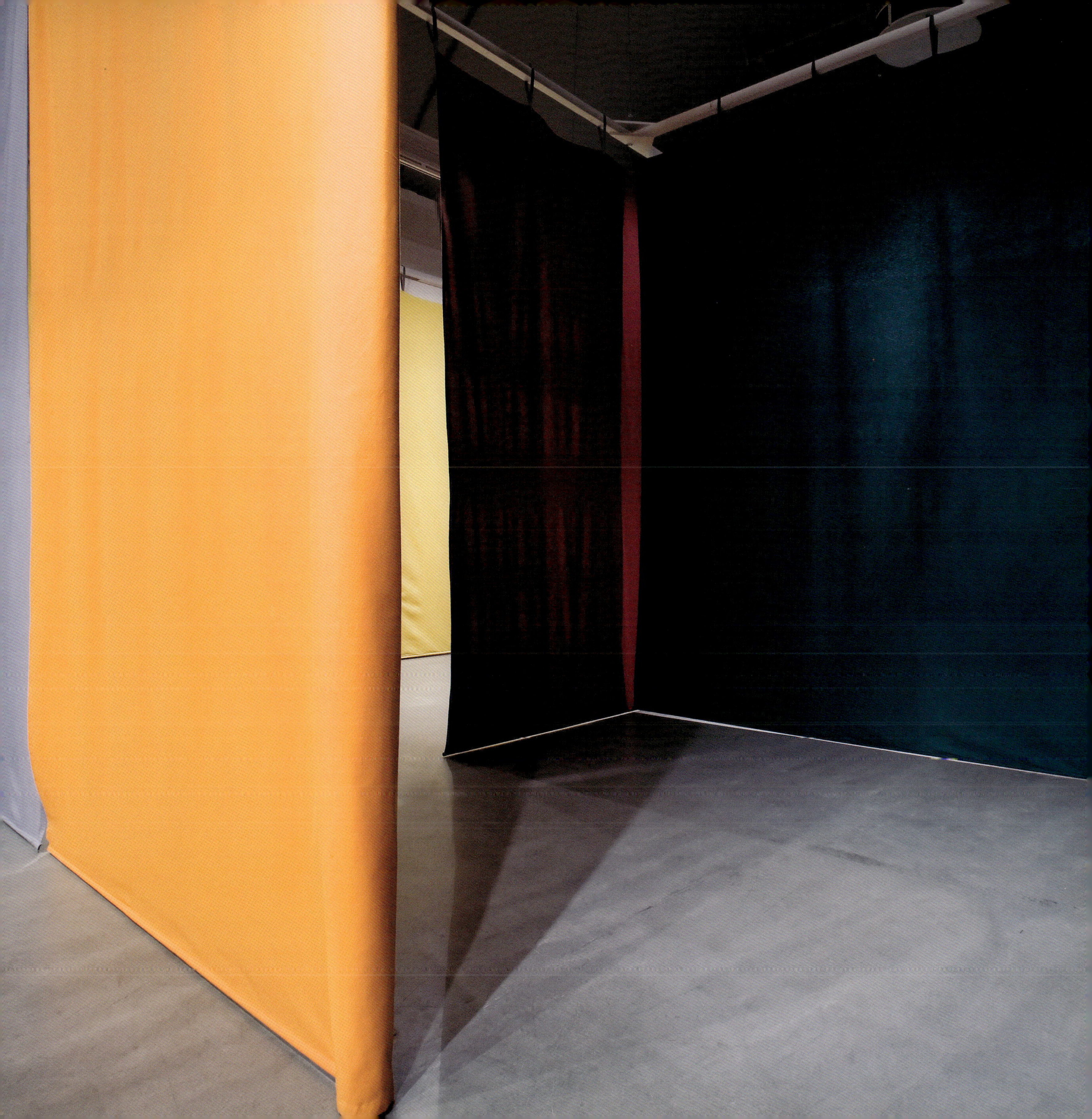

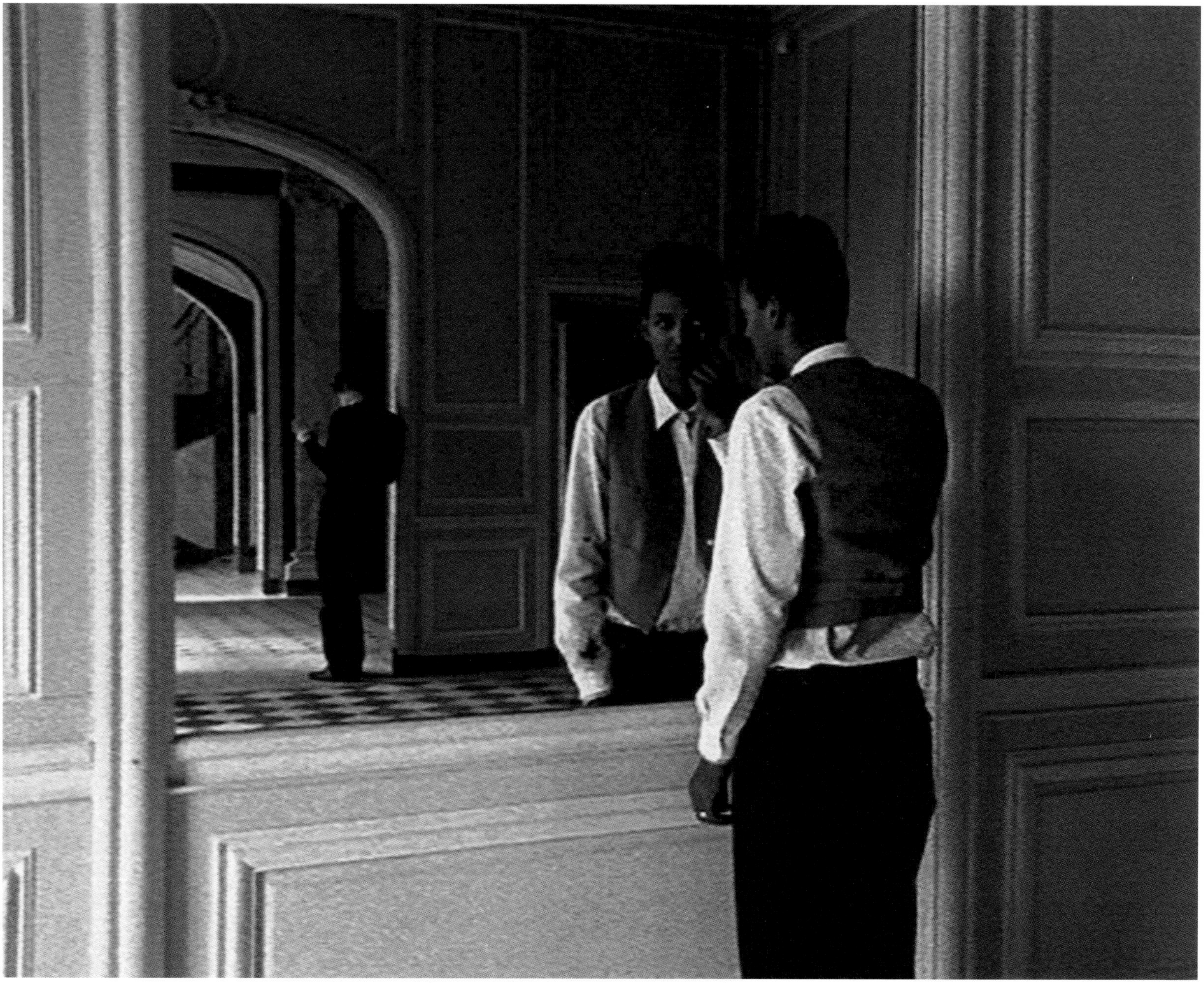

Stills from *8*, 2007

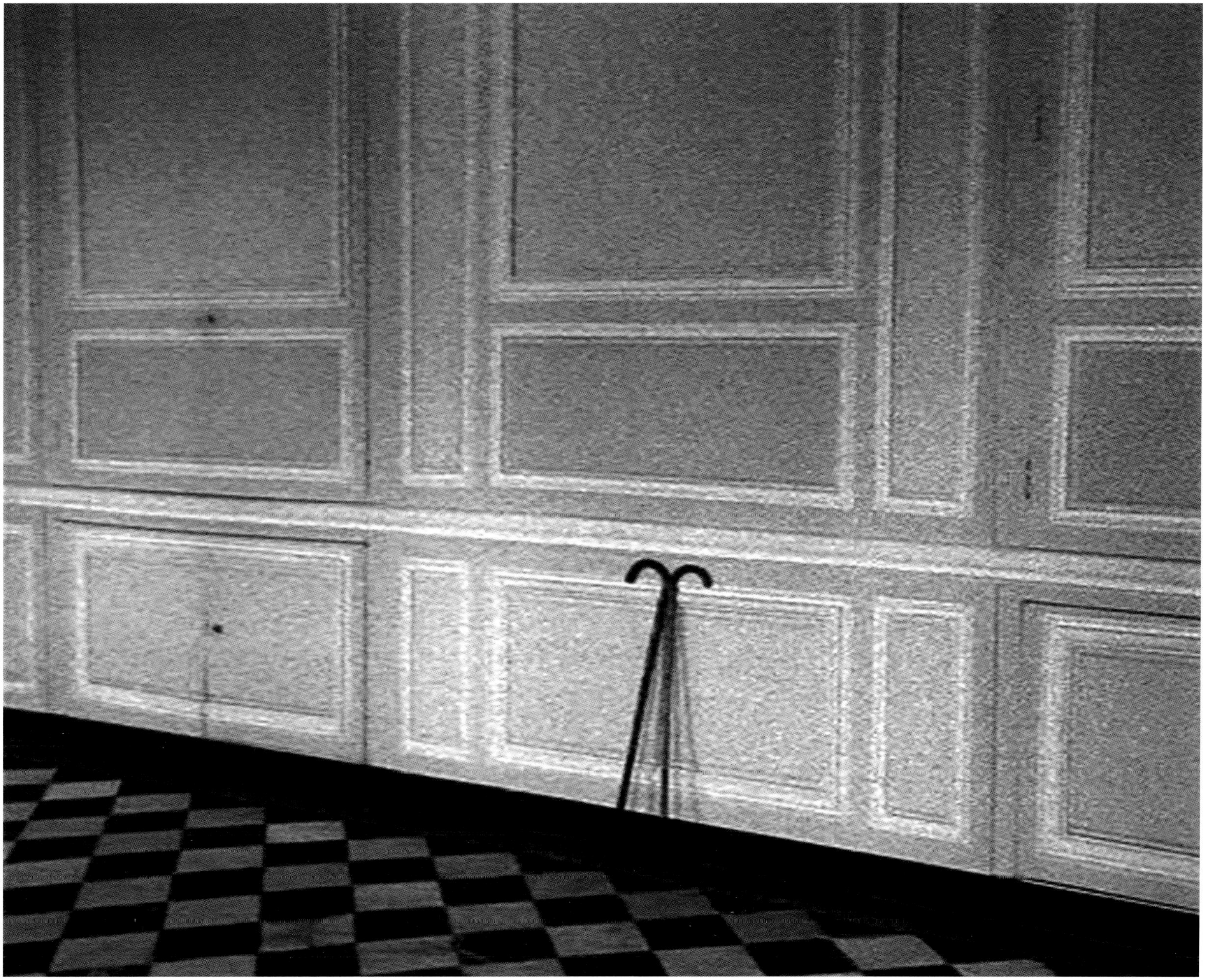

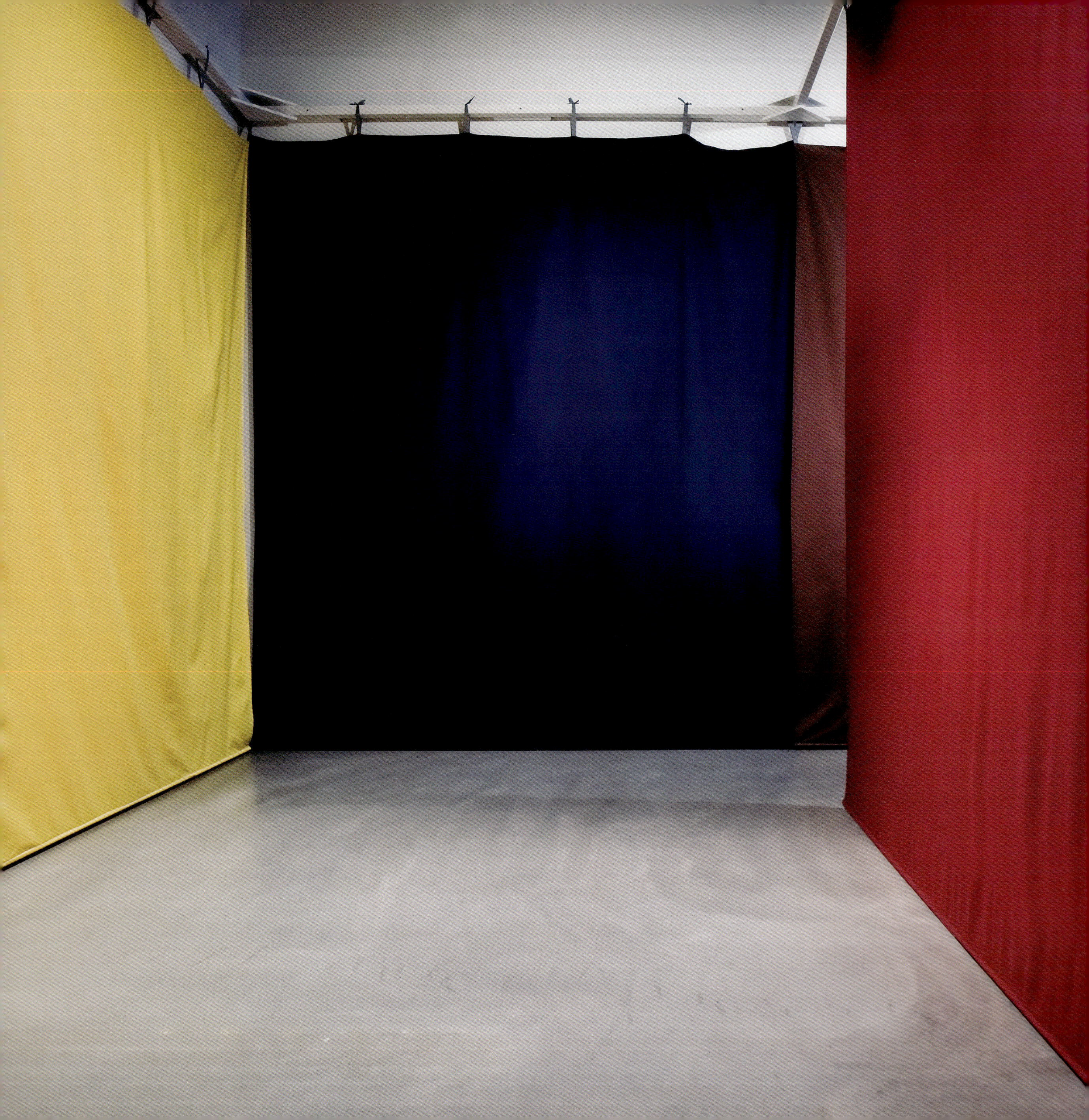

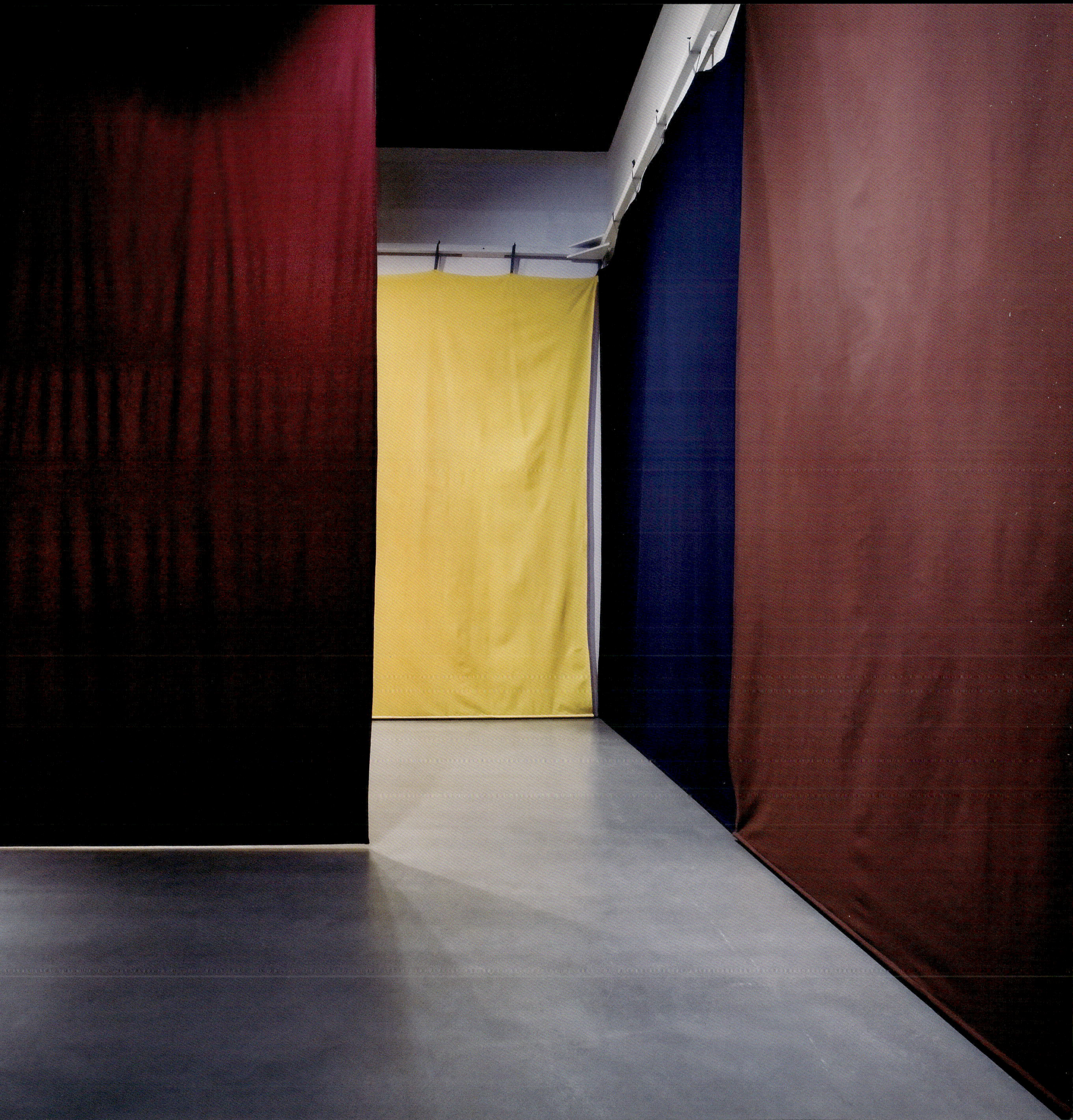

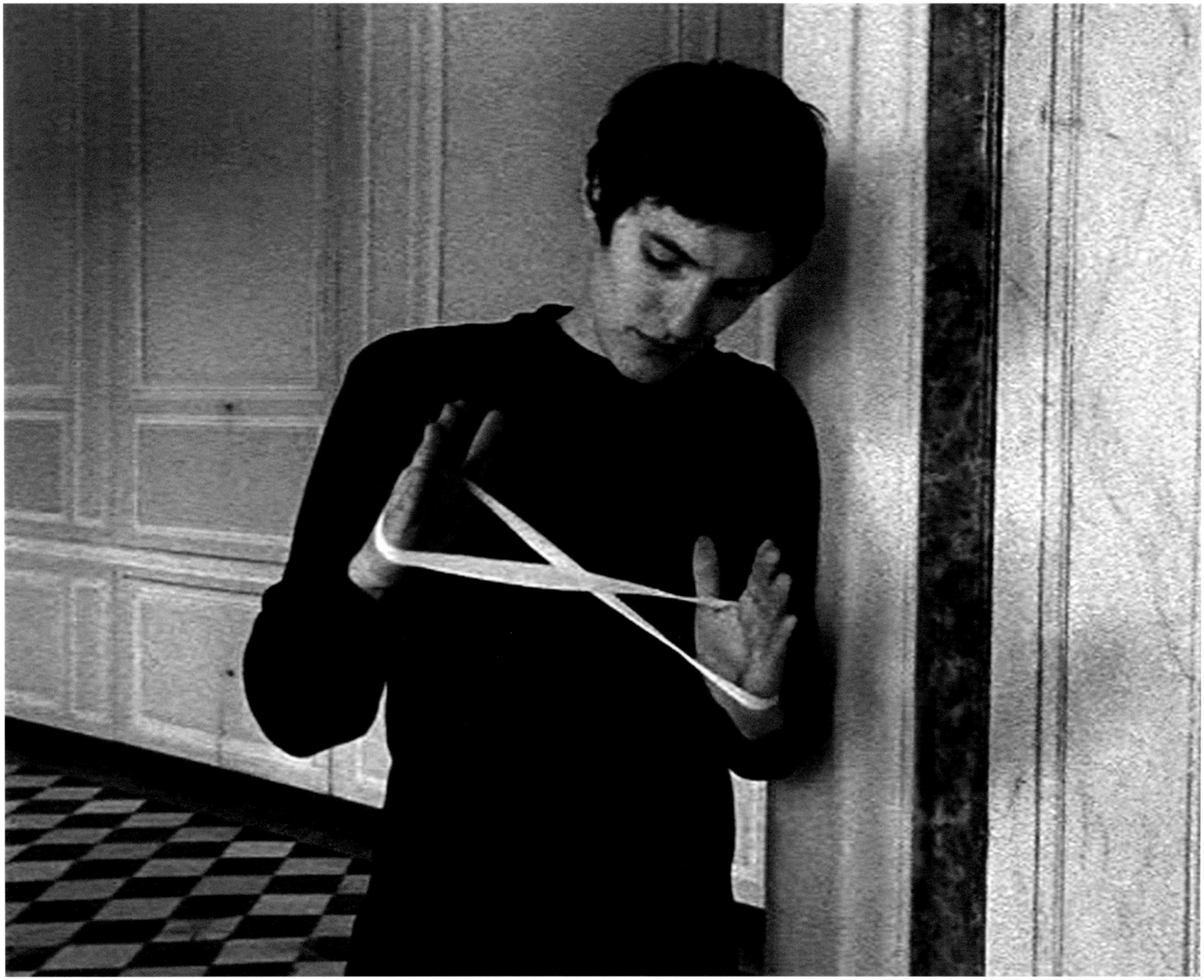

Stills from *8*, 2007

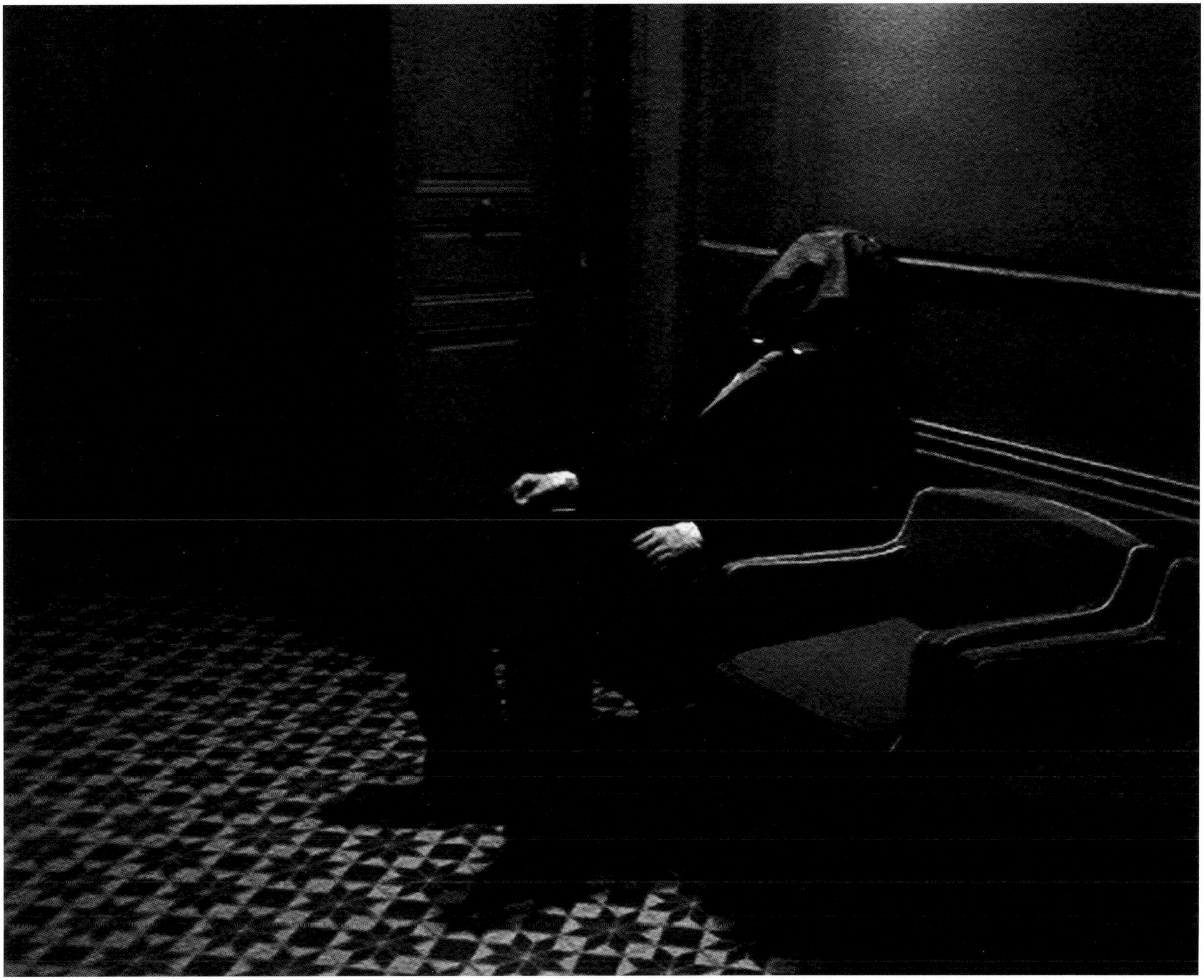

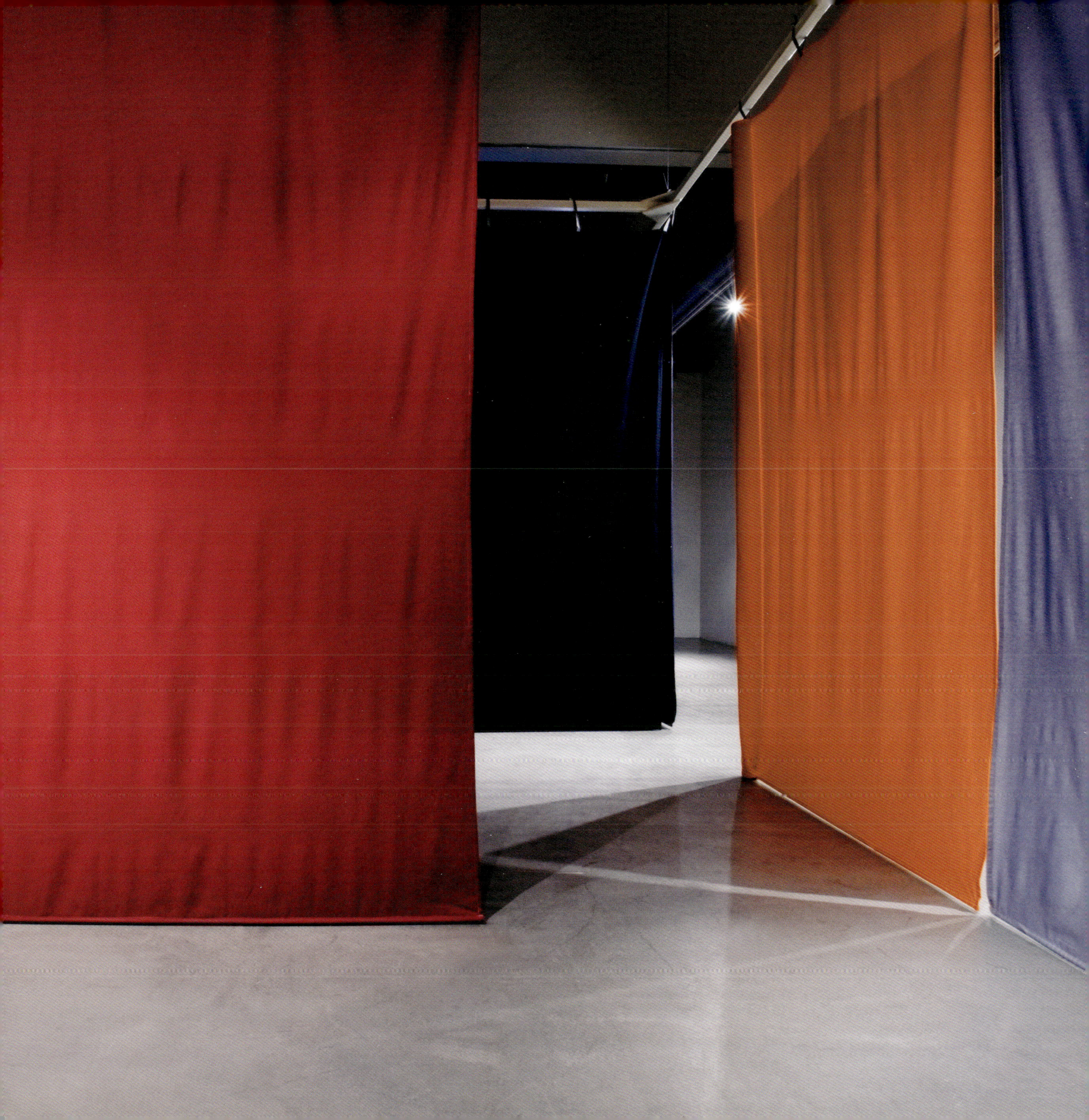

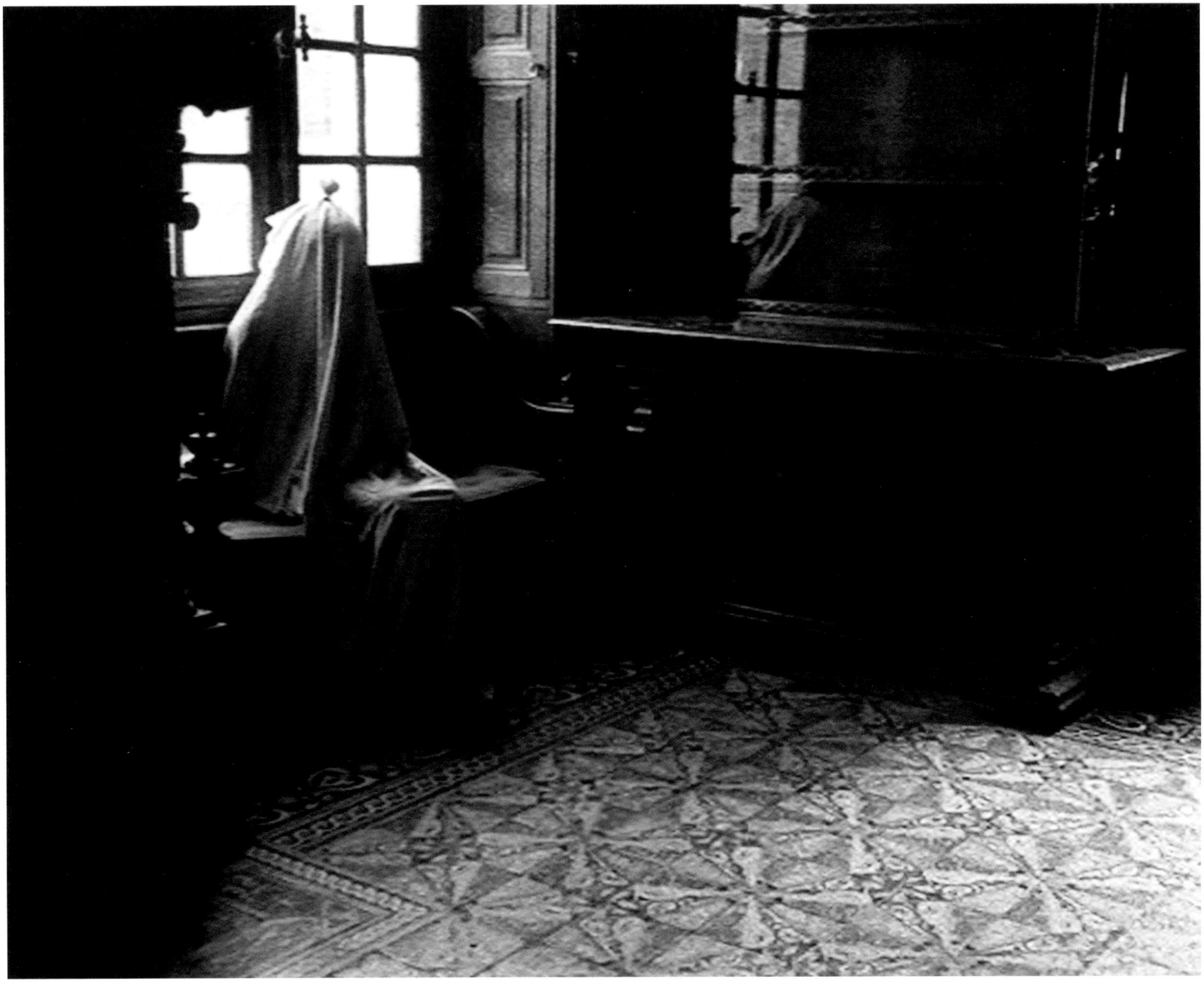

Stills from *8*, 2007

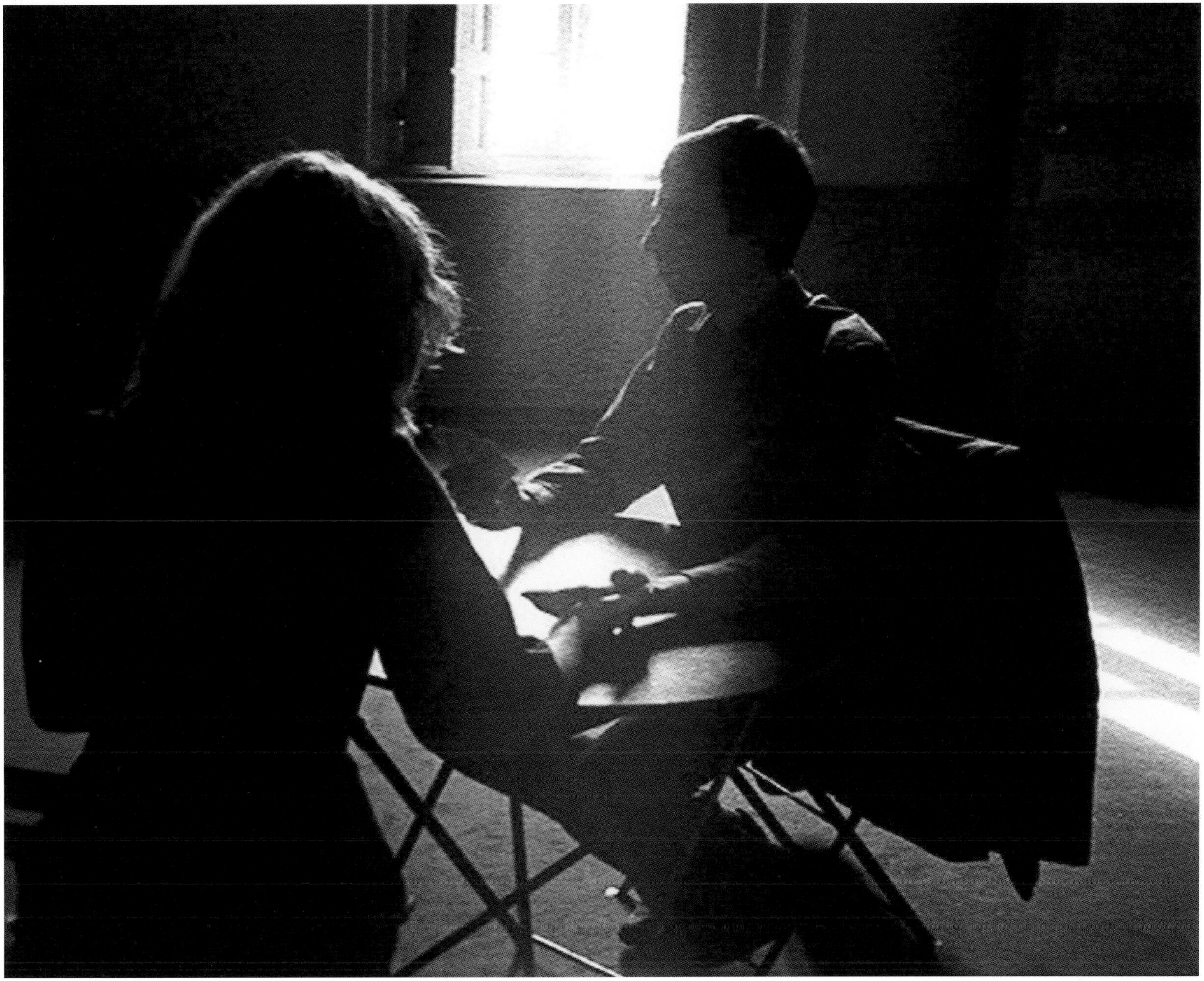

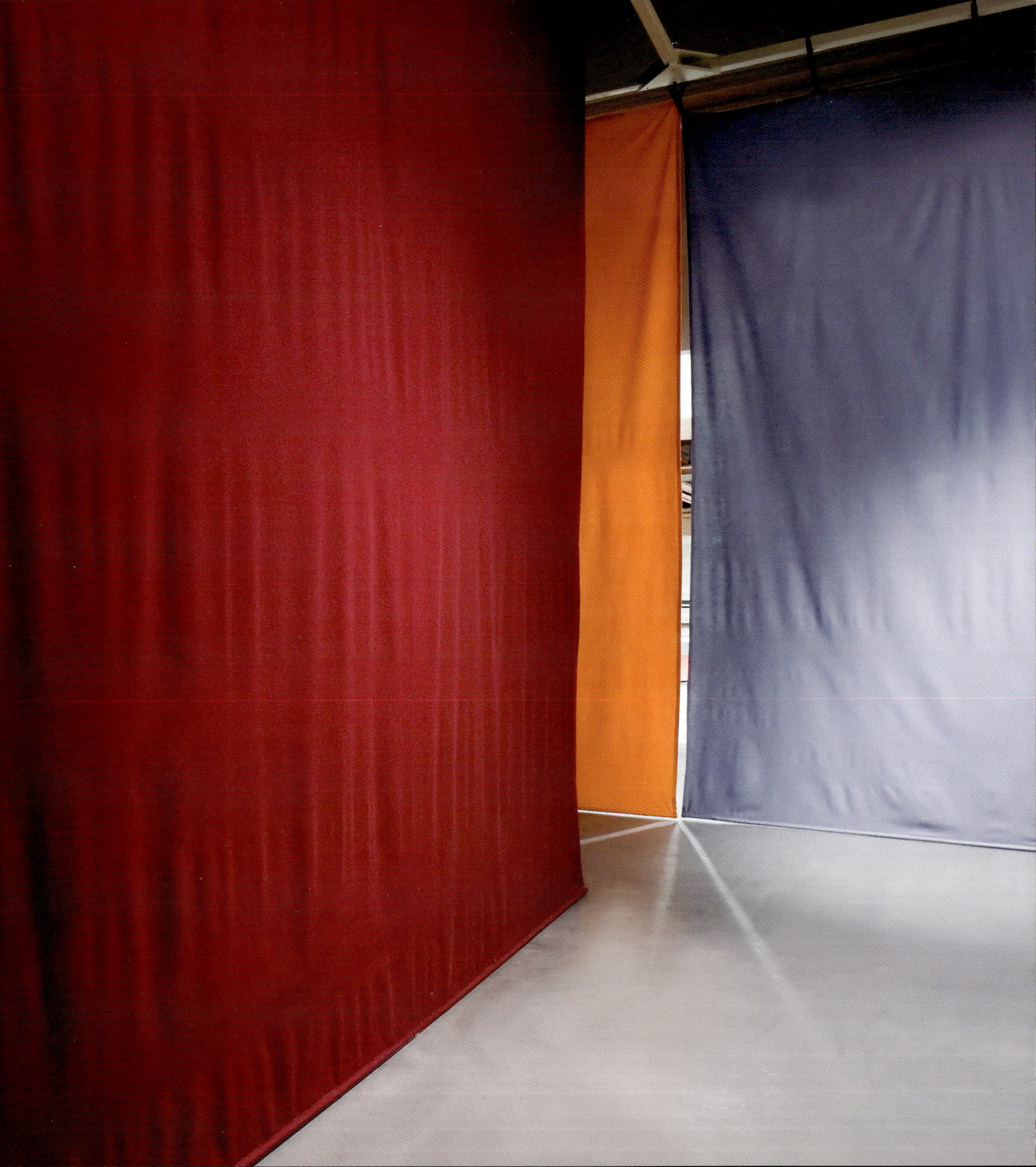

List of Illustrations
Selected Biography
Acknowledgements

List of Illustrations

Kugel (Ball)
16mm film, B&W, silent, looped,
2 min 46 sec
2007
Dimensions: variable
Courtesy: The artist, Art:Concept, Paris and Produzentengalerie, Hamburg
Installation shot: '*World as a Stage*', Tate Modern, London, 2007
Film stills:
Edition of 5
Page number: 40, 43

Geist (Ghost) *
16mm film, b&w, silent, looped,
1 min 5 sec
2007
Dimensions: variable
Courtesy: The artist, Art:Concept, Paris and Produzentengalerie, Hamburg
Film still
Edition of 5
Page number: 41—42

Quilt
Watercolour, collage
2005
200 × 150 cm
Courtesy: The artist and Produzentengalerie, Hamburg
Photo credit: Peter Sander, Hamburg
Page number: 44

Karo Sieben (Seven of Diamonds) *
Tinted fabric on wooden plinth, walking sticks, rope
2007
4.85 × 4.21 × 0.1 m
Courtesy: The artist and Art:Concept, Paris
Photo credit: Fabrice Gousset
Installation shot: Ulla von Brandenburg, Karo Sieben, Art:Concept, Paris (Detail)
Page number: 44, 48, 49, 50

Ein Seltsames Fest – Schattenspiel (An Unusual Party – Shadowplay, with Julia Horstmann)
Cutouts behind curtain, slide projector, text, sound
Performance: Kunstverein Braunschweig
2005
Dimensions: Variable
Courtesy: The artist and Julia Horstmann
Photo credit: Laurent Montaron
Page number: 51, 52

Tarot: 7 d' épeé (7 of Swords)
Screen-print on paper
2008
78 cards, each: 120 × 63 mm
Design: Clemens Habicht
Courtesy: The artist and IMMA, Dublin
Edition of 100
Page number: 65

8 *
16mm film, B&W, silent, looped
8 min 10 sec
2007
Dimensions: Variable
Courtesy: The artist, Art:Concept, Paris and Produzentengalerie, Hamburg
Edition of 5
Page number: 66, 67, 70, 71, 74, 75, 78, 79

8
Cotton curtains and 16mm film
2008
Dimensions: Variable
Installation shots: 'La Maison', Docking Station, Stedelijk Museum Amsterdam
Courtesy: Art:Concept, Paris and Produzentengalerie, Hamburg
Photo credit: Gert Jan van Rooij
Page number: 68, 69, 72, 73, 76, 77, 80

Tarot Set *
Screen-print on paper
2008
78 cards, each: 120 × 63 mm
Design: Clemens Habicht
Courtesy: The artist and IMMA, Dublin
Edition of 100
Page number: 86—87

* works included in the exhibition at the Irish Museum of Modern Art

Works in the exhibition that are not inculded in this catalogue

Curtain
Tinted cotton
2008
Dimensions variable
Courtesy: The artist

Mann mit Fellhut (Man with Fur Hat)
Watercolour on tissue paper
2008
147 × 114 cm
Courtesy: The artist
Photo credit: Yun Lee

Matrose (Sailor)
Watercolour on tissue paper
2008
Dimensions: 147 × 114 cm
Courtesy: The artist
Photo credit: Yun Lee

Schauspieler 1 (Actor 1)
Watercolour on tissue paper
2008
147 × 114 cm
Courtesy: The artist
Photo credit: Yun Lee

Schauspieler 2 (Actor 2)
Watercolour on tissue paper
2008
147 × 114 cm
Courtesy: The artist
Photo credit: Yun Lee

Paar (Couple)
Watercolour on tissue paper
2008
147 × 114 cm
Courtesy: The artist
Photo credit: Yun Lee

Selected Biography

Ulla von BRANDENBURG
born in 1974 in Karlsruhe, Germany
Graduated from Ecole des Beaux-Arts de Hamburg, Germany
Lives and works in Hamburg and Paris

Solo Exhibitions :

2008
Project PS1, New York, USA
Irish Museum of Modern Art, Dublin, Ireland
CCA Wattis Institute for Contemporary Arts, San Francisco, USA
Kunsthalle, Düsseldorf, Germany
Docking Station, Project Space, Stedelijk Museum, Amsterdam, Netherlands

2007
Karo Sieben, Art: Concept, Paris, France
Brief Oder Neuigkeiten (Letter or News), Produzentengalerie, Hamburg, Germany

2006
Cinq milliards d'années, Palais de Tokyo, Paris, France
Kunsthalle, Zürich, Switzerland

2005
I Am Making a Crazy Quilt and I Want Your Face for the Center, Pavilion Project, Montreal, Canada
Fuenf sind's doch schon im ersten Spiel, Trottoir, Hamburg, Germany

2004
Ein Mensch ist keine Nadel, Blaue Kugel Hamburg, Germany
Ouija, Diplomausstellung HfbK, Hamburg, Germany

2003
Den Gelben in die Ecke, Doublette in der Mitte, Studiogalerie, Kunstverein Braunschweig, Germany

2001
Ja. Auch Sie!, Galerie Taubenstraße, Hamburg, Germany

Group Exhibitions:

2008
Biennale Jérusalem, Israel
Biennale Bucharest, Romania
Wizard of Oz, CCA Wattis Institute for Contemporary Arts, San Francisco, USA
Biennale Sydney, Australia
The World as a Stage, ICA, Boston, USA
5 min later, Kunstwerke, Berlin, Germany

2007
Mask, James Cohan Gallery, New York, USA
Re-Mission, Liebling, Berlin, Germany
Collector, Point Ephemere, Paris, France
Performa07, the 2nd Visual Art Performance Biennal, New York, USA
The World as a Stage, Tate Modern, London, UK
stand Art : Concept, Frieze, London, UK
House Trip, Artforum Berlin, Germany
Le Jour et la Nuit, Parc culturel de Rentilly, Bussy-Saint-Martin, France
Like Leaves, Tanya Bonakdar Gallery, New York, USA
Le Truc, Project Arts Center, Dublin, Ireland
Against Time, Bonniers Konsthall, Stockholm, Sweden
Continuous Project Altered Monthly, CCA Wattis Institute for Contemporary Arts, San Francisco, USA
Pale Carnage, Dundee Contemporary Arts, Dundee, UK
RE-DIS-PLAY, Heildelberger Kunstverein, Heidelberg, Germany
Tanzen – Sehen, Centro Andaluz de Arte Contemporáneo, Sevilla, Spain
PRAGUEBIENNALE3 : Expanding Painting 2, Prague, Czech Republic
Time out of Joint, FRAC Aquitaine, Bordeaux, France
bookish relations, Bibliothekswohnung, Berlin, Germany
Café Moskau, Berlin, Germany
LEMAITRE: Électrons libres, Tabacalera Donostia, Saint Sebastian, Spain
Kunstpreis der Böttcherstrasse in Bremen, Kunsthalle Bremen, Germany
Re-trait, Fondation d'Entreprise Ricard, Paris, France
Les roses de Jericho, attitudes, Geneva, Switzerland
Surface Wave, Foxy Production, New York, USA
No More Boring Art, Point Éphémère, Paris, France
Tanzen – Sehen, Museum für Gegenwartskunst, Siegen, Germany
INSERT 1, Kunstverein, Hamburg, Germany
Armory Show, New York, USA
Pale Carnage, Arnolfini Gallery, Bristol, UK
Inky Toys Affinitas, CerealArt Project Room, Philadelphia, USA
Kunstverein, Hamburg, Germany

2006
ART'FAB, Saint Tropez, France
Premier Jour, Irma VepLab, Châtillon-sur-Marne, France
Deutsche Wandstuecke, Sette scene di nuova pittura germanica, Museion, Bolzano, Italy
Groupshow, Palais für aktuelle Kunst, Glückstadt, Germany
Again for Tomorrow, Royal College of Art, London, UK
Motor Immobile, Greene Naftali, New York, USA
Bonanza, Jack Tilton, New York, USA
As if by Magic, Art Center / South Florida, Miami Beach, USA
Stipendium, Kunstverein, Hamburg, Germany

2005
Don't Accept Manana, Kunstverein Braunschweig, Germany
Neue Freunde, Kunstverein Schwaz, Österreich, Germany
I Still Believe in Miracles, ARC Musée d'Art Moderne de la ville de, Paris, France
Jahresgaben 2005, Kunstverein, Braunschweig, Germany
Jahresgaben 2005, Kunstverein, Schwaz, Germany

2004
Deutschland sucht, Kunstverein, Cologne, Germany
Provide it, Halle für Kunst, Lüneburg, Germany
Jahresgaben 2004, Kunstverein, Braunschweig, Germany
Jahresgaben 2004, Kunstverein, Cologne, Germany
Nobody, Der Graue Zylinder, Merrettich Pavillion, Berlin, Germany
Index, Kunsthaus, Hamburg, Germany
Sammlung Taubenstrasse, Kunsthaus, Hamburg, Germany
Ouija, Diplomausstellung HfbK, Hamburg, Germany

2003
Feine Ware 3, Kunstverein, Hamburg, Germany
Reward, Blueroom Gallery, London, UK
Zimmer aufräumen, Zupfgeigenhansel kommt, Künstlerhaus Stuttgart, Kunstverein Dresden, Germany

2002
Slow, Shedhalle, Zurich, Switzerland
Jahresgaben 2002, Kunstverein, Braunschweig, Germany

2001
Wir, Comawoche, Klasse Cosima von Bonin, Hamburg, Germany

2000
Die jüngere Generation, Orgelfabrik Karlsruhe Durlach, Germany
Neue Blicke, Neue Räume, Schauspielhaus Hamburg, Germany

1999
Voices, ZKM Karlsruhe, Germany

1998
5 Jahre HfG, HfG Karlsruhe, Germany

Performances:

2007
Performance Schattenspiel, Bonniers Konsthall, Stockholm, Sweden

2006
Performance, Liste 06, Art Basel, Switzerland

2005
What you are, we were; What we are, you will be, Art Basel Miami, USA
La Regle du Jeu, Kunstverein Braunschweig, Germany
Ein Seltsames Fest, Kunstverein Braunschweig, Germany
Danse de l'ombre, Kunstverein Schwaz, Germany

2004
Performance Perfekt, Die Blaue Kugel Gruppe, Halle für Kunst, Lüneburg, Germany

2003
Zimmer aufräumen, Zupfgeigenhansel kommt, HfbK Hamburg, Germany
Kunstverein Dresden, Künstlerhaus, Stuttgart, Germany

2002
Alles Roger Commander, Cosima von Bonin, Kunstverein Hamburg, Germany
Planche, Klasse Cosima von Bonin, HfbK, Hamburg, Germany

Publications:

Group Exhibition Catalogues:

2007
Ulla von Brandenburg, 'Key,' *Anachronisms, Against Time*, Bonniers Konsthall, WS Bookwell, Finland
Hoffmann, Jens, 'Ulla von Brandenburg,' *Ice Cream*, Phaidon : London, UK
'Ulla von Brandenburg,' *Electrons Libres*, Tabacalera Donostia, Spain
Sdun, Nora, 'Gesellschaftstänze – Ulla von Brandenburg,' *Kunstpreis der Böttcherstrasse*, Bremen, Kunsthalle Bremen, Germany
Pale Carnage, Bristol : Arnolfini, UK
Don't Accept Manana, Kunstverein Braunschweig, Frankfurt Main : Revolver, Germany

2006
Deutsche Wandstücke, Sette Scene di Nuova Pittura Germanica, Museion, Bolzano, Milan, Italy
Creambook 2006, Phaidon : London, UK
Stipendium, Kunstverein Hamburg, Germany

2005
Möntmann, Nina, *I Still Believe in Miracles*, ARC/Musee d'art moderne, Paris, France
Die Blaue Kugel, *Vite Vite Verlag*, Hamburg, Germany

2004
Nr.2, artist journal by Ulla von Brandenburg, offset print
Spur 04. The Cheap Champagne Issue, Materialverlag, Hamburg, Germany
Auf der Suche nach dem verlorenen Bahnhof, Das Dreckige Butzend
Deutschland Sucht, Kunstverein Köln, Germany

2002
5 Jahre Galerie Taubenstrasse, Hamburg, Germany
Shedhalle 2002, Shedhalle Zürich, Switzerland
Abracadabra, artist journal by Ulla von Brandenburg, silkscreen print

2000
Neue Blicke, Neue Räume, Schauspielhaus, Hamburg, Germany

1998
5 Jahre HfG, HfG Karlsruhe, Germany

Solo Exhibition Catalogues:

Ulla von Brandenburg – Brief oder Neuigkeiten, Produzentengalerie Hamburg, Germany, 2007
Ulla von Brandenburg, Künstlerstätte Schloss Bleckede, 2006
Ulla von Brandenburg, Kunstverein Braunschweig, 2005

Prizes:

2007
Kunstpreis der Böttcherstrasse in Bremen

2006
Juergen-Ponto-Stipendium

2005
Reisestipendium, Verein für Neue Kunst, Hamburg
Stipendium Künstlerstätte Schloss Bleckede

2003
Begabtenstipendium der Dietzte-Stiftung

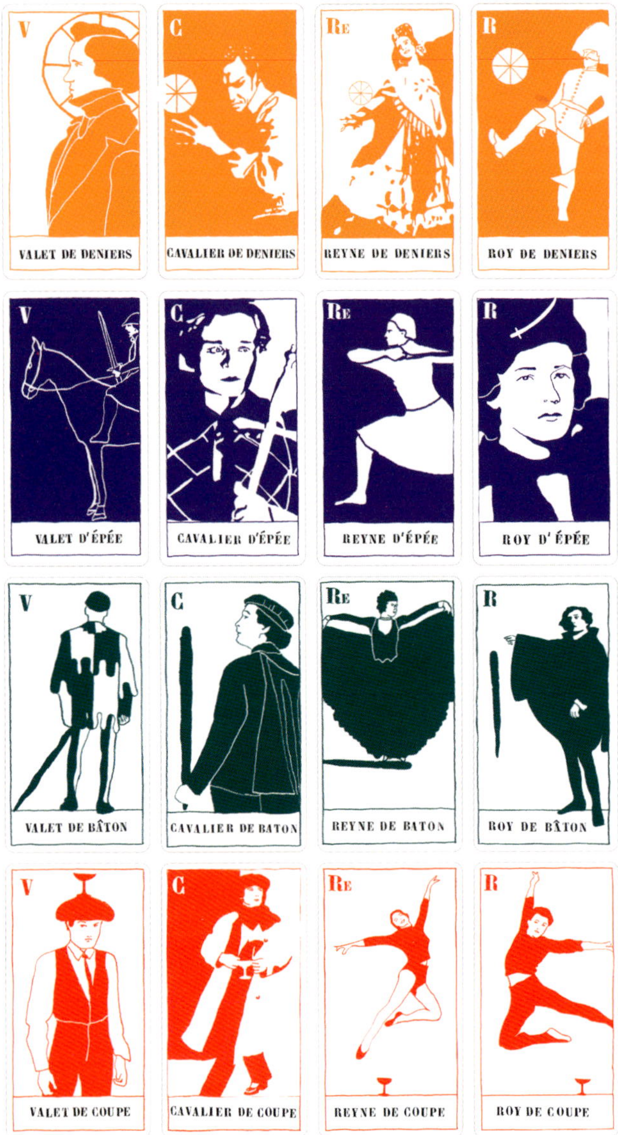

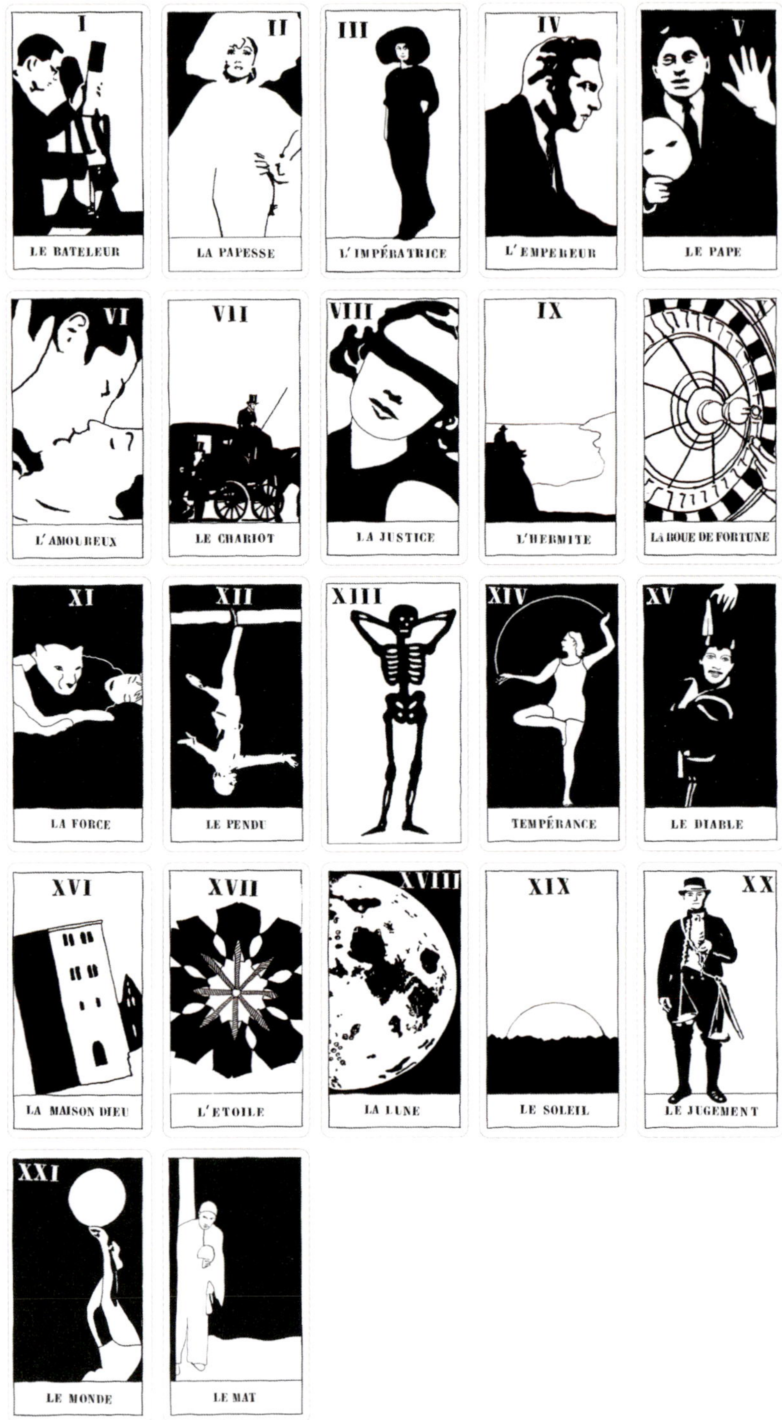

Tarot set, 2008

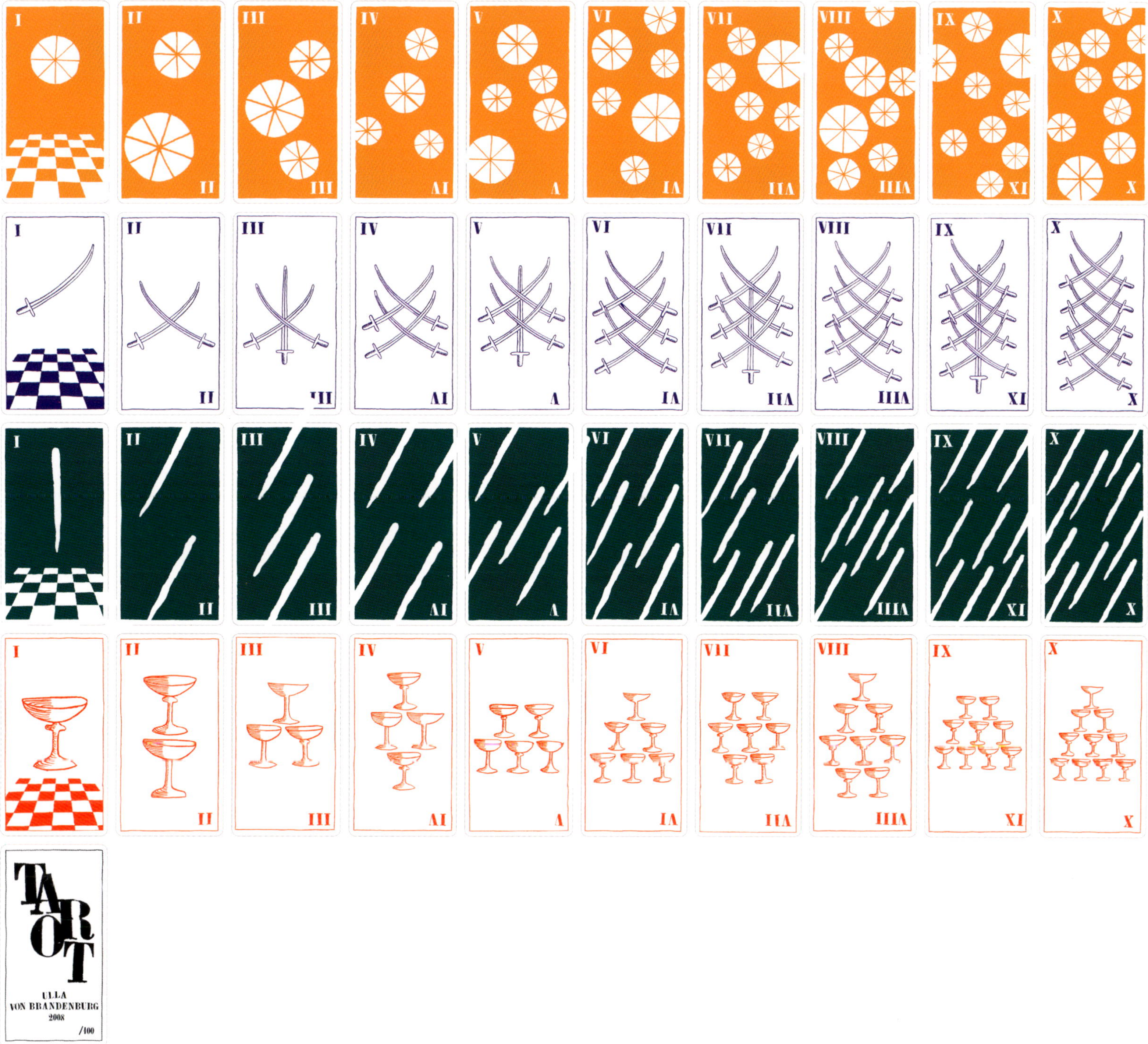
TAROT
ULLA
VON BRANDENBURG
2008
/100

Acknowledgements

IMMA would like to thank Ulla von Brandenburg, Art:Concept, Paris, Produzentengalerie, Hamburg, Pilar Corrias Ltd, London and Goethe-Institute, Dublin for supporting this publication.

We would also like to thank both the artist's studios and assistant Malin Pettersson Oberg, Nicholas Vargelis and Clemens Habicht. without whom the production of new commissions would not have been possible.

The artist wishes to thank Enrique Juncosa, Rachael Thomas, Nicola Lees, Scott Williams, Henrik Kubel, Georgina Jackson, Charlotte Bonham-Carter, Beatrix Ruf, Declan Long, Lindsey Hanlon, Art:Concept, Laurent Montaron, Produzentengalerie and all the participants of 'Kugel' and '8' which was produced by ADN Factory, Paris

Art:Concept, Paris
Produzentengalerie, Hamburg
Pilar Corrias, London

GOETHE-INSTITUT
DUBLIN

Supporting IMMA

Honorary Patrons

Maurice and Maire Foley
George McClelland
Gerard O'Toole
Lochlann and Brenda Quinn

Patrons

Brian and Elsa Ranalow
Eoin and Patricia McGonigal
John Reynolds
Joe Christle
Colm Quigley (Horwath Bastow Charleton)
Mairead and Finbar Cahill
Anne Lyons (Jefferson Smurfit Trustees)
Moya Doherty and John McColgan (Abhann)
Derville Murphy (Bank of Ireland)
Ivor Fitzpatrick (Ivor Fitzpatrick & Co)
Maureen O'Driscoll-Levy
Beth Davies Ryan (Diageo)
Noel Smyth

Benefactors

Stelio Marcos Amarante
Eileen and Paul Bowman
Brennan Insurance
Diarmuid Brennan
Campbell Bruce and Jackie Stanley
Frank X. Buckley
Dr Abdul Bulbulia
Maeve Callanan
Philip Carton
Michael Corrigan and Mary Kilcullen
Brian Coyle
John Daly
Grainne Dooley
Bernard Dunleavy
Siobhan Fahy
Lorna Fitzsimons
Tom E. Honan
Suzanne MacDougald
Margaret McGlynn
Loretto Meagher
Belinda Moller
Carmel Naughton
James and Marion O'Driscoll
Cormac O'Malley
Gearóid Ó Súilleabháin
Michael O'Sullivan
Maureen Porteous